Parting Sense

A Complete Guide To Divorce Mediation

Jack J. Shapiro

Marla S. Caplan

All rights reserved. No part of this book may be reproduced in any form or by any electronic or mechanical means including information storage and retrieval systems, except brief passages by a reviewer without written permission from the publisher.

Published by:
Greenspring Publications
#3 Barstad Court
Lutherville, Maryland 21093

Distributed by:
Liberty Publishing Company, Inc.
50 Scott Adam Road
Cockeysville, Maryland 21030

© Jack J. Shapiro and Marla S. Caplan, 1983, 1986

Library of Congress #83-82885
ISBN 0-89709-146-9

Manufactured USA

*Dedicated
in memoriam to*
O. J. COOGLER
*friend, teacher,
sage.*

TABLE OF CONTENTS

Foreword	1
Preface	3
The Sense of Mediation	7
Why mediate? What are the emotional and financial benefits?	
The Practice of Mediation	19
Who can do the job? How do you do it?	
Temporary Settlement Agreement	31
How important is it?	
The Property Settlement	37
Who gets what? How are debts paid?	
Financial Support	61
What will my financial needs be? Will I need money for the children?	
Children and Custody	71
What's best for the children? We can *both* have custody?	
Taxes and Divorce	83
How can I avoid capital gains tax? What's deductible? What's not? Who's entitled to the exemption?	
The Agreement	91
Putting it all together.	
Some Final Thoughts	99
Appendices	105
Footnotes	129
References	131
Index	133

FOREWORD

Mediation for couples contemplating separation or divorce is a new service. To date there are no guides for the consumer to use in selecting a properly qualified professional. Such guidance is greatly needed, especially in an emerging field like Family Mediation.

Jack J. Shapiro, a practicing attorney and mediator in Baltimore, Maryland, has impressed me with the knowledge, sensitivity and compassion that he brings to families facing the trauma of separation and divorce. Having refused in his legal practice to represent one party in an adversarial divorce, he has become one of the most dedicated proponents of family mediation to date. A frequent speaker and teacher on mediation, he has influenced the growth of the movement and brought knowledge of a better way to resolve family problems to many.

His book is, to my knowledge, the first attempt to explain the practice of mediation to consumers, and should be considered a must for those who wish to use mediation in their divorce settlement.

O. J. Coogler

PREFACE

Marriages are ending! In dramatically increasing numbers and for a wide variety of reasons, Americans are divorcing. Until recently, this choice has meant legal confrontation. In these circumstances, spouses become adversarial enemies, pitted against one another, in an expensive win-lose divorce battle that is often open to public scrutiny. When this occurs, parents and children alike are exposed to enormous stress, often far more devastating to the family than whatever caused the breakup in the first place. Indeed, is there anyone left in the land who has not heard the plaintive cry of a friend or relative suffering the agony of adversarial divorce?

Necessity, it is said, is often the mother of invention; and, in the last several years a new approach to separation and divorce has emerged which promises a vast improvement in the way divorce is treated in our country. This approach recognizes that divorce need not take place on the legal battlefield and that treating one's spouse like an enemy is not a prerequisite for ending a marital relationship. This process is known as divorce mediation.

Mediation, unlike adversarial confrontation, stresses rational cooperation. As a result, conflict is minimized. Similarly, the cost and the time necessary to reach a divorce settlement are minimized. Because the spouses focus their energies on solving the practical problems they face, mediation achieves fair divorce settlements. Most important, mediation discourages couples from wallowing in the kind of destructive and non-productive thinking that is so typical of adversarial divorce, (such as, "the more I hurt my ex-spouse, the better off I'll be.").

One of the purposes of this *Guide*, therefore, is to acquaint its readers with the concept and practice of divorce mediation. We will try to answer the numerous questions associated with this process, so that couples may make better informed decisions about how they wish to obtain a divorce settlement.

An additional purpose of *Parting Sense* is to introduce its readers to the concept of joint custody and to describe how it works. Traditional adversarial divorce typically treats children like property, so that when a marriage ends, children are awarded as property is awarded, to one spouse or the other. In such circumstances, the non-custodial parent is essentially stripped of his or her parenthood. Visitation is often a hollow substitute for legitimate parenting. Recently, state legislatures, notably in California, have begun to recognize that it is not in the best interests of children to deny them what was essentially a birthright—two parents. Joint custody and why recent research findings make consideration of the joint custody option so important will be discussed.

Our final purpose is to suggest that family relationships do not necessarily end upon divorce, particularly where children are involved. Certainly, the family relationship is restructured, but not terminated. If spouses can keep this in mind, as they mediate their divorce settlement, parent-child relationships as well as effective co-parenting will be protected and nurtured. Understanding this, we believe, will enable a separating couple to maximize their new relationships and the new support system which has been created.

Parting Sense portrays various husband and wife relationships which help us illustrate certain aspects of the mediation process. The danger inherent in such portrayals is that some readers may mistakenly believe that this stereotypes certain social roles. We assure you that this is not the case. Our examples are derived from the experience of working with numerous couples in mediation, and every effort has been made to describe mediation in an objective, unbiased fashion based on these experiences.

Additionally, some words about how to read our book may be helpful. *Parting Sense* is a guide for couples who believe that mediation may offer a useful alternative in their divorce transition. It should not be thought of as a textbook which dictates how mediation will actually occur or which requires intense study to make mediation successful. Some parts of the *Guide* may seem complicated, especially that portion relating to property settlements. Don't let this overwhelm you. Our purpose is to sufficiently discuss mediation so that you may feel comfortable with it, not to make you proficient practicing mediators. In other words, take our *Guide* seriously, but not too seriously. Treat it as you might a good wine; know it well enough to appreciate it, but don't worry about growing the grapes in your own backyard.

In parting, divorce mediation has now proven itself to be a valid and important alternative to adversarial divorce. It has worked successfully for rich and poor alike. Based on this evidence, it is now clear that mediation has survived its infancy, and will continue to play an increasingly important role in our social fabric. We hope that *Parting Sense* will, in some small measure, aid that cause.

J. S.

M. C.

THE SENSE OF MEDIATION

The Decision To Separate

The choice to separate is never an easy one. Normally, the decision is made after months, if not years, of difficult soul searching. Often, the decision is not made mutually by the marriage partners. As a result, either the husband or wife is surprised and emotionally hurt by the unilateral choice of his or her mate to leave the marriage relationship. Yet, experience has taught that the commitment of two persons is necessary if a marriage is to survive and work. If one spouse is truly committed to a separation, there is little the other spouse can do to preserve the marriage.

It is at the moment of disclosure, and shortly after, that the marriage partners are most vulnerable to adversarial divorce. Typically, one spouse or the other seeks the services of a lawyer, as much to vent his or her anger and hurt, as to obtain protection of his rights. From that moment forward two persons, who once cared very much for one another, are thrust into a system of reprisal and conflict that rarely, if ever, produces a "winner" in family disputes.

Mediation, instead of confrontation, is now a choice which couples have when ending marriage relationships. To those of us who practice mediation, it is clear that mediation works when both members of a couple recognize and accept (perhaps with resignation) that the marriage relationship is over. Furthermore, they must be willing to put aside their immediate emotional pain in recognition that a cooperative approach to divorce better serves their family's long and short term needs and interests.

We expect this book to be read, partly, by persons who are genuinely concerned about their marital relationship, but who have not, as yet, made a firm decision to divorce. To those who find themselves in this position, we strongly recommend a gentle and reasonable course, and urge you to make every effort to reconcile your marital differences. When this is not possible, however, every effort should be made to minimize the emotional and financial consequences of a future separation.

Reactions by one spouse to the disclosure by the other of a desire to separate are many and varied, and there is no foolproof method of insuring a cooperative, rather than an adversarial, approach to divorce. We can say with assurance, however, that significant numbers of couples have chosen mediation because, in the final analysis, it just makes sense.

Divorce Mediation Defined

Divorce mediation may be defined as a process of direct negotiations between spouses who are terminating a marriage. A neutral third party, a mediator, participates in the negotiations to help the spouses achieve fair and equitable agreements. The areas which the spouses discuss include, but are not limited to:

1. Division of marital property
2. Spousal support

3. Child custody and parental access
4. Child support
5. Tax considerations

Mediation's purpose, therefore, is to help the spouses come to mutually acceptable and fair agreements that are very practical in nature, and touch upon all of the important issues that divorcing couples must consider. They are precisely the same matters which would be dealt with by the lawyers in an adversarial divorce.

Mediation specifically empowers the spouses to act on their own behalf; that is, they, and not their legal representatives, are the negotiators in the process. Sometimes, people are at first frightened by the thought of negotiating for themselves. However, when they understand the mediation process and the safeguards within that process, they become more comfortable with mediation. In addition, it is important to note that if the couple chooses adversarial divorce, they are, in effect empowering a judge or a master to impose on them the judge's or master's ideas about fairness. In adversarial divorce, the spouses relinquish control over their own lives, and more than one observer has characterized this process as 'little more than an expensive roll of the dice.'

Mediation works because the spouses themselves must and do invest their efforts to make it work. As a result of this joint participation, a lasting equitable agreement emerges, tailored by the couple to meet the specific needs of their restructured family.

Uses of Mediation

There are actually three distinct situations which may appropriately utilize mediation. Briefly stated, they are:

1. When a couple desires a trial separation;
2. When a couple desires a permanent separation and divorce;
3. When a couple is divorced, but because of changed circumstances, wishes to renegotiate and modify the terms of their settlement.

This book is primarily directed to the second circumstance; however, the other two situations should not be overlooked for mediation purposes.

Trial separations are of course exactly what the name implies; a chance for the spouses to independently review their marital relationship without committing themselves to a formal separation. Trial separations, however, like formal separations, require careful planning and often appropriate bargaining and compromise. Mediation serves this purpose well.

Similarly, mediation is also very useful when a couple has obtained a divorce but, because of changed circumstances, want to renegotiate the terms of their settlement. Child custody, child support and spousal support are usually the areas discussed.

The Emotional Sense

When two people decide to marry, each makes an enormous emotional investment in the other. In effect, they say to one another, I believe you are capable of lending me your support in helping to make life's rough spots more tolerable and life generally more worthwhile and fulfilling. Similarly, I want to be there to help you over the rough spots and to help make your life more worthwhile and fulfilling. This mutual commitment forges the emotional and psychological interconnections in a marriage. The feelings each spouse has because of these interconnections, run deep.

As a result of the depth of feelings that spouses often have during the course of separation, the emotional process of separation and divorce can be, and often is, highly charged. Anger, fear, bitterness, intense loneliness and frustration can be but some of the emotions triggered by separation and divorce. We know that these emotions can create roadblocks that keep spouses from doing what they inevitably must do; become independent both emotionally and economically. We also know of the adverse effects that parental bitterness, anger and fear can have on children.[1]

Without question, adversarial divorce fuels the fires of the harsh emotions which are already present in the divorce transition. It is not that lawyers seek or want such results; rather, they and their clients are locked into a system which necessarily escalates conflict. For example, in order to persuade a judge or master that his client should be awarded custody of a child, the lawyer is compelled to prove the lack of fitness of the other spouse to be the custodial parent. Moreover, litigation incorrectly implies that one party will win and one party will lose, based on who was "at fault" for the breakup of the marriage.

There are no "winners" when a child is forced to see his parents trying to prove that the other is incompetent, or when two spouses who once loved one another, hold one another's flaws and vulnerabilities out for public scrutiny. Such a setting, is emotional quicksand for all involved. It is not surprising that a family often emerges from the divorce more shattered by the experience of the adversarial process itself, than by whatever caused the divorce in the first place.

The alternative to adversarial divorce is mediation. It is specifically designed and implemented to minimize conflict and thus to calm the harsh emotional consequences that people experience. To begin with, the concept of "fault" is abandoned. Historically, courts would grant a divorce only if one spouse was found to be legally blameworthy or "at fault." Fault charges often focus on desertion and/or adultery. Today, we recognize that marriages end for a variety of complex and interrelated reasons. This is why 48 out of 50 states recognize "no-fault" divorce. This means that couples can be granted a divorce without blaming either party. Thus, there is no longer the need to "destroy" one's former marriage partner. Mediation adopts the "no-fault" basis for divorce.

Unlike litigation, mediation encourages a constructive, continuing dialogue between the spouses themselves. In this way they are each able to gain meaningful insights into each other's concerns and needs. Such mutual understandings clearly reduce the emotional pain that is otherwise present, and enable the spouses to create a settlement agreement that meets their emotional as well as their practical requirements. The following example illustrates this.

During mediation, it became clear that after the separation, Dianne, while comfortable, would not have the financial resources that her husband Bill would have. Dianne felt vulnerable in terms of her ability to make material gifts to the children, particularly vacations, compared to Bill's ability to do so. Because the couple was in mediation, Dianne could and did express her concerns to her husband. Shortly thereafter, Bill acknowledged Dianne's concerns and stated that he would abide by an unwritten rule not to compete with Dianne for the children's affections by showering them with material gifts. Consider for a moment, not only the benefits obtained by Dianne, but also the fact that the children have been protected from inappropriate parental competition.

As we said earlier, mediation is a self-empowering process; that is, the spouses take responsibility for their own futures rather than relinquish such responsibility to lawyers and judges. Since the spouses are required to actively participate in planning their futures, it is that much easier to put aside the pain of the past. The very experience of taking control works to overcome the emotional helplessness so often associated with divorce and creates a constructive rather than a destructive environment in which spouses can move forward with their lives.

The Practical Sense

Once a couple has decided to mediate their divorce, their first task is to identify a mediator who is acceptable to both husband and wife. Later, we will discuss how to go about locating such a person, but for now, suffice it to say that the usual practice, once a mediator is tentatively identified, is to arrange for an initial one hour mediation session. At this session, the mediator fully explains the mediation process, his or her fee schedule, and uses the opportunity to explore the issues which will need to be negotiated as a result of the particular circumstances presented by the couple. In marked contrast to an adversarial divorce, by the end of the first session, the couple and the mediator have a sense of what lies ahead.

The cost of mediation services varies from mediator to mediator; most mediators charge a fee in the range of $50-$100 per hour. A total fee of between $500 and $1,000 can be anticipated based on 10-15 hours of work, and this may include the services of a consulting attorney who drafts the proposed marital settlement agreement and who makes necessary legal information available to the spouses so that fully informed decisions are made.

In comparison, when the adversarial method of divorce is used, it is not uncommon for each spouse to pay an initial retainer fee of at least $500 against an hourly charge of $75-$125. A total bill for legal services of between $3,000 and $5,000 is often incurred and these figures may be exceeded. The cost benefit of mediation, therefore, is readily apparent.

Time is another factor that deserves attention. Mediation generally can be concluded within two months of the first working session. In contrast, adversarial divorce is rarely concluded within six months and often will exceed a year. If the spouses must go the full litigation route, a two year period is not uncommon and then, only if appeals are not taken.

Also, when divorces are litigated, spouses frequently return to court, time and again, in order to obtain modifications to the decree and modifications of the modifications. It is not uncommon for the process to go on for years. By contrast, couples who mediate their divorces are much more likely to adhere to their original agreements because they, and not a third party, made them. When changes in circumstances do occur which make modifications to the original decree appropriate, such changes are usually resolved through mutually acceptable mediation efforts.[2]

In summary, mediation provides a rational, humane alternative to adversarial divorce. The process has enormous emotional and practical advantages over adversarial divorce and is available to any couple who can resist the temptation to use divorce as a means of recrimination and punishment. As a judge in Maryland recently said: "It is the divorce process of the eighties."[3] We would add, 'and beyond.'

The Decision To Mediate

Here, we introduce you to Beth and David Malone, a fictitious couple, who, with us, will travel a mediation journey to a divorce settlement. In various portions of this book, Beth and David will meet their mediator, Paul, to discuss their mediation work.

Beth and David are 40 and 42 years of age respectively. They have been married for 16 years and have two children, Chris and Billy, ages 14 and 11.

Dave, since graduating from college with a Master's degree in business administration, worked first as an account executive for a large insurance brokerage firm. Five years ago, he left his job with the insurance agency to begin his own insurance business. In the last two years, the business has performed very well.

Beth, prior to marrying Dave, taught special education in public school and supported Dave, including paying the tuition for his Master's program. Soon after Dave's graduation, Beth stopped working in order to have and care for the couple's children. For the past several years, Beth has been able to devote some time to substitute teaching, earning a few thousand dollars each year.

Beth and Dave, having sensed problems in their marriage, worked with a marriage counselor for several months. They then began a one month's trial separation. The agreement regarding the trial separation had been worked out with the help of Paul, a divorce mediator, who was recommended by their marriage counselor. The trial separation helped make it clear to both Dave and Beth that a legal separation was what they wanted.

Beth and Dave had been urged by family and friends not to mediate their divorce, but rather to immediately hire lawyers and file suit for divorce. Both had been told repeatedly that they would have to "fight it out" to get what is their "just due."

They are now with Paul at the orientation session. The conversation that follows is a condensed version of a portion of the session.

Dave: I hear what you are saying, Paul, about how much money mediation will cost and how long it will take and that sounds good, but what good does it do me if I don't get the best deal that I can?

Paul (Mediator): Beth, you must also want the best deal you can get, just like Dave. Is that correct?

Beth: Sure, I want a fair deal.

Paul (Mediator): Now that's interesting, Beth. You said a fair deal. Is that what you want, a fair deal?

Beth: Yes, a fair deal. I want what is fair.

Paul (Mediator): Dave, do you think there is a difference between the best deal you can get and a fair deal?

Dave: That's a good question. Look, I don't want to bury Beth, but a lot has gone down and she is the one who wanted out. Why should I go to the poor house?

Paul (Mediator): Wait a minute! First I hear Dave say he doesn't want to bury Beth and I hear Beth say she wants a fair deal. Dave, let me ask you a question. Is it important to tell why your marriage has ended to the whole world in court?

Dave: No, I really don't want to get into that. It's not that I have anything to hide or be ashamed of, but Beth is right, nobody's perfect.

Paul (Mediator): O.K., nobody is perfect and you don't want to bury Beth.

Dave: Right.

Paul (Mediator): Well, isn't the way to avoid this dilemma to see what you each think is fair and agree to it if you can? After we're finished, you each have the right to ask your own lawyers if they think the agreement is fair, before you sign on the dotted line. Couples who have used this method have had very positive results. The agreements hold because they are fair. Does that make sense to you?

Dave: I see your point.

Beth: It makes sense to me and we haven't even discussed what is best for the children.

Dave: Oh God, they have been through so much already. It would kill me to make them see us slug it out in court.

Paul (Mediator): Look folks, it is my practice not to ask for a commitment to mediate at the orientation session. This is an important decision and you'll want to think about it. If mediation makes sense to you, give me a call and we'll set up our first session. O.K.?

Beth and Dave: O.K.

THE PRACTICE OF MEDIATION

A new profession has been born—that of family mediator. This new profession has come to exist because of our great need to establish an alternative to adversarial divorce. In Chapter Two, we will look at the professional mediator and describe the way in which he relates to his clients. Our discussion begins, however, with a description of a document known as a "Marital Settlement Agreement." The work of the couple and mediator has always as its goal, the creation and formal acceptance of this document.

A Contract and More

The marriage contract is widely understood; it is a social contract made between husband and wife establishing the marriage relationship within commonly accepted social norms. When a couple elects to end a marriage, however, they typically enter into another contract. This one, unlike the marriage contract, is in writing, signed by the parties, usually notarized and details at length the agreements made between the spouses ending their marriage relationship. This contract is commonly referred to as a "Marital Settlement Agreement."

The entire purpose of mediation is to achieve understandings between the spouses which are then incorporated into a "Marital Settlement Agreement." This agreement later becomes the basis for a divorce decree signed by a judge. When the decree is signed by a judge and entered by a clerk of the court into the court's records, the marriage is legally over and the spouses are free to remarry if they choose to do so.

Unlike other contracts, however, most if not all states give the courts the right to modify the terms of a Marital Settlement Agreement in certain specified areas. Child custody, child support, and spousal support are normally these areas. The safeguards built into the mediation process (i.e. a well trained mediator, an independent attorney review, etc.) decrease the probability of judicial modifications.

To allow you to gain some familiarity with a Marital Settlement Agreement, we have included Beth and Dave's agreement (see "The Agreement" chapter). Readers are cautioned that this is an example only, and as such, it should be used solely for educational purposes. This agreement should never be a model for the reader's personal use. Readers are further cautioned that marital settlement agreements must be drafted by experienced lawyers familiar with the laws of the state in which a divorce will be obtained. Mediation recognizes and incorporates this practice.

We suggest that you carefully review Beth and Dave's agreement. You may, however, find it helpful to read the entire *Guide* first. In this way, Beth and Dave's mediation experience will enable you to have a more complete understanding of their marital settlement agreement, and you will be able to see how the document incorporates their work in mediation.

The Mediator

Marital settlement agreements are based on agreements which the spouses reach in the following areas: (1)

property, (2) spousal support, (3) child support, (4) child custody and parental visitation and (5) tax considerations. Decisions in these areas are very practical ones. It is the function of the mediator to help the spouses make fair and equitable decisions with regard to each. Later in the book, these areas will be explored in depth. Our purpose now is to demonstrate the way the mediator interacts with a couple and to present the typical ground rules that exist between the mediator and a couple. In this regard, it would be useful, first, to profile the professional mediator.

Most (but not all) mediators come from either legal or mental health professions (family counselors, psychologists or social workers). Lawyers, as a result of their training, are highly sensitive to the dynamics of negotiation; mental health professionals, as a result of their training, are highly skilled in interpersonal communication. Clearly, both professions serve mediation well.

Mediation, however, is not lawyering or mental health counseling. The mediator is not a legal representative of either one or both spouses, nor does the mediator provide therapy. The function of the mediator is to help the spouses achieve a fair bargain in the context of available family resources. In this role, the mediator does not judge the spouses or attempt to impose any particular results on them. The spouses themselves are the negotiators in the process and no solution will be accepted until they, through their own efforts, create solutions with which they are both comfortable. The mediator skillfully guides the spouses through an exhaustive search for fair results, but it is always the spouses themselves who negotiate and who finally reach agreement.

While mediators do not impose their own concepts of fairness on the spouses, they do try to keep the spouses' discussions about fairness within appropriate limits. We know that long term, voluntary adherence to agreements must survive the immediate emotional impact of the separation and divorce. Sometimes, the emotions felt by couples who mediate their divorces have a tendency to unbalance the negotiations. For example, either the husband or wife may come to mediation with feelings of guilt that for the moment elicit a wholesale giveaway. The immediate result may be a quick fix for the guilt, but it also insures long term dissatisfaction with the bargain and an ultimate breakdown in the agreement. The mediator strives to prevent this, and may diplomatically intervene in the negotiations to keep them in proper balance.

Mediator Training and Experience

The training and experience of a mediator is a legitimate concern for any couple contemplating mediation. This is especially so because no state, local jurisdiction or private organization presently certifies mediators. Anyone, therefore, is free to call himself a divorce or family mediator.

This is not to say that consumers of mediation services cannot make intelligent decisions about the person with whom they choose to work. It does mean that couples must be assertive enough to ask questions and firm enough not to be distracted from getting the answers they deserve.

Mediation requires a strong professional background either in law or the social sciences; but a degree alone in either of these fields is not sufficient. In addition to proper educational training, mediators must have substantial practical experience beyond their degree. Furthermore, successful completion of a comprehensive training program specifically in divorce mediation is necessary. Of course, there is no substitute for experience and couples are urged to find mediators with divorce mediation experience, in addition to appropriate training. In considering a mediator, ask how many mediations he or she has performed and whether any previous clients are willing to discuss their mediation experience. Finding a qualified mediator may take effort and perseverance, but it will not be time wasted.

Neutrality

A mediator must scrupulously maintain neutrality during the mediation process and couples who wish to mediate their separation and divorce must begin their search for a mediator with this as a first priority. If neutrality is not genuinely perceived by both husband and wife throughout the mediation process, mediation will fail. Should either spouse ever question the mediator's neutrality, this issue must be openly discussed, and if any doubt remains, the mediation must terminate and another mediator be found.

Neutrality, however, extends beyond the mediator and applies to any other professional who may become involved in the divorce. For example, if a pension or a business interest requires financial analysis or if a house must be appraised, the accountants and real estate appraisers chosen to do the work should exhibit the same neutral posture as the mediator.

Confidentiality

Unlike courtroom proceedings, which are open to the public, mediation takes place in a highly private and confidential environment. Furthermore, mediators will usually ask the couple to agree not to discuss their mediation with anyone who is not involved in it and particularly not with friends or relatives. Such communication, with nonparticipants, has a tendency to disrupt the negotiations and create confusion in the minds of the spouses. The preferred policy is to wait until a proposed marital settlement agreement is drafted, but not signed, and then have the spouses discuss its terms with anyone they choose, prior to signing the final agreement. Under these circumstances, the entire agreement can be reviewed for fairness, rather than isolated segments, which may not present a clear picture of the fairness of the entire agreement.

Full Disclosure

The spouses must come to mediation prepared to make full disclosure of all their individual and joint financial affairs. The importance of full disclosure cannot be overstated. Again, the obligation to make full disclosure is contained in the mediator-client agreement.

Couples can expect that the mediator will want to review the previous two or three years' income tax returns, as well as all financial statements supplied to banks or other lending institutions during the same period. One of the functions of the mediator is to review these documents in order to insure that full disclosure has taken place. One may expect a complete set of financial records to be requested for the mediator and each spouse. If at any time during the mediation process, there exists some indication that full disclosure has not been made by either of the spouses, then the mediation must be terminated or suspended until disclosure is made.

Moreover, marital settlement agreements normally contain warranties of full disclosure, and thus, if full disclosure has not been made by both spouses, the agreement becomes subject to attack. Of course, every effort must be made to avoid such a result.

Methods of Mediation

Mediation is not practiced uniformly throughout the United States. There are, in this regard, three variations in method that deserve explanation. Couples may have preferences among these methods and it is our purpose to describe them so that better informed choices regarding mediation may be made. The variations involve: (1) the use of legal counsel; (2) co-mediation; and (3) joint mediation versus the "shuttle" method.

The Use of Legal Counsel

Divorce is both a social process and a legal process. It is a legal process because the authority of the court must be invoked to finally and fully end a marriage. Also, marital settlement agreements are contracts which must be prepared by lawyers. It is clear, therefore, that mediation must employ an attorney's skill and knowledge at various points along its course. There are options about how this is done, and it is our purpose to describe them here.

One method that is practiced involves the use of an

advisory attorney. Usually, this person is someone the mediator has suggested because the mediator has confidence in the attorney's knowledge of family law. The functions of the advisory attorney are to make legal information available to the couple so they can make informed decisions about their separation and divorce and to prepare the couple's marital settlement agreement in proper legal form. The advisory attorney does not represent the individual interests of either the husband or wife.

The fact that the advisory attorney is utilized, may discourage each of the spouses from consulting with independent attorneys of their choice to review the proposed marital settlement agreement before it is signed. Experience has demonstrated to us, however, that such a review is an important and valid part of the mediation process. Typically, such a review consists of two to three hours of attorney time. On occasion, a couple will return for an additional mediation session to discuss their attorney's comments or modify the agreement because of their attorney's concerns. When the agreement meets with the approval of independent attorneys, the confidence the couple feels in their agreement is magnified.

Co-Mediation

Normally, a couple works with one mediator. An alternative approach, however, is for the couple to meet with two mediators and when this occurs, it is known as co-mediation.

Co-mediation may be preferred by a couple in order to establish a sexual or professional balancing between the mediators. One spouse or the other may feel more comfortable working with at least one mediator of their sex. Similarly, it is sometimes helpful to use two mediators, one with a background in law and one with a background in counseling or mental health.

Couples should understand that costs are naturally increased when co-mediation is used, but the option is often available. Couples who desire co-mediation should inquire about the previous co-mediation experience of the mediators under consideration. Co-mediation requires good teamwork and this is derived from previous co-mediation experience.

Joint Mediation Versus The "Shuttle" Method
Another alternative couples have who are considering mediation concerns whether mediation sessions will be held with husband, wife and mediator present at all times (i.e. joint mediation), or whether the mediator alternately meets with husband, then wife, and so forth (i.e. the "shuttle" method).

Because mediation is generally regarded as an opportunity for the spouses to begin establishing a cooperative post-divorce relationship, most mediators currently use the joint mediation approach.

Some mediators, particularly those with backgrounds in labor mediation, use the "shuttle" method. Indeed, this may be particularly attractive to people who do not want an adversarial divorce, but whose emotions are running too high to permit discussions to occur in the same room, at the same time.

The Mediator-Client Agreement

In most instances, mediators and their clients establish a contractual relationship through a written agreement. This document describes the functions performed by the mediator and establishes certain criteria for the mediation process. Beth and Dave's agreement with Paul is found in Appendix A. Below, we discuss several specific aspects of this agreement which require some explanation. They are, in a sense, the mediation ground rules.

The Mediation Guidelines

Other than the mediator, nothing is more significant to mediation than the mediation guidelines. These guidelines create the framework for the negotiations which follow. Any couple considering mediation must carefully review them. We are confident that such a review will assure the reader that the guidelines will achieve *fair* results for husband and wife alike. The guidelines can be found in Appendix B.

While later chapters will examine the guidelines in depth, it is appropriate here to discuss two aspects of the guidelines, which relate to marital property and spousal support. These two matters deserve attention because they reflect significant changes in the way society, and thus our legal system, has viewed an evolving change in husband and wife relationships and the status of women in society.

Many, if not most, states have recognized these changes. However, even if your state has not adopted them, you may still use the guidelines for mediation purposes. In effect, the guidelines become a private agreement between the couple to help them reach a fair settlement.

The first matter involves the concept of **marital property**. Under the mediation guidelines, marital property is all property acquired by husband or wife, individually or jointly, during their marital relationship. The only exception is property received as a gift or inheritance by one spouse, but not the other. Marital property is not affected by the manner in which property is titled, or by who provided the funds to acquire the property.

This view is based upon the belief that a wife, whose labors have maintained a household and cared for the day-to-day needs of the family's children, has contributed to the accumulation of property to the same extent as her husband who has made a contribution through employment. The wife's efforts, in effect, permit the husband to work rather than care for the house and family needs. Marriage is seen as a full partnership in which both husband and wife share equally.

This concept replaces the previous notion that the titling of property and the monetary contribution to the accumulation of property determines the division of a couple's property in a divorce.

The second aspect of the guidelines worth highlighting concerns spousal support. Under the guidelines, there is no presumption that a husband has a lifelong duty to support his wife. Rather, the guidelines are constructed so that the spouses pull themselves away from financial dependence as soon as is practically possible. In most instances, this results in an exploration in mediation of the wife's ability to work or to return to school to increase her employable skills. Spousal support by the husband, therefore, is measured, in part, by the wife's ability to earn an independent income, and may be limited in amount and/or time, accordingly. Again, the guidelines have incorporated what is clearly the evolutionary direction society has taken in the areas of women's rights, responsibilities and equality of position with men in society.

The importance of each spouse carefully reviewing the guidelines cannot be overstated. They are clear guideposts to fair results, and if adhered to, will achieve such results for husband and wife alike.

THE TEMPORARY SETTLEMENT AGREEMENT

Once a couple has made a decision to mediate their separation, the terms of a temporary settlement agreement often become their first mediation objective. Usually, the couple or one of the spouses, is feeling extremely stressed by their living circumstances and feels a strong need to create separate living arrangements for themselves. Often, but not always, a couple privately decides which of them will leave the marital home, but they may be concerned about the legal consequences of such a decision. One of the risks a couple takes when one spouse leaves the marital home involves the possibility of a charge of desertion sometime in the future. Therefore, the first purpose of the temporary settlement agreement is to clearly state that the couple is separating by mutual and voluntary consent. The significance here is twofold. First, the adverse possibility of a charge of desertion has been removed. Second, because neither party is blaming the other for the divorce, an equality of position has been established between the spouses. This, in turn, permits them to focus on constructive problem solving.

In addition to stating that the separation was by mutual and voluntary consent, the temporary settlement agreement may also establish agreements pertaining to finances and child custody. That is, the couple may agree to temporary spousal and child support. They may also include decisions concerning where the child will live and visitation arrangements. Sometimes, the agreement will even specify how and when a spouse will leave the family home, who will assist in the move and which property will be taken.

Beth and Dave are now with Paul to discuss whether they need a temporary settlement agreement. Their discussions, of course, are in condensed form.

Paul (Mediator): As I indicated to you at our orientation session, one of the first things we need to discuss is your desire to physically separate, whether this is something you want to do now, or whether you want to wait until the final agreement is signed.

Beth: I guess you can understand that things haven't been too good around the house. Emotions are running high and that's bad for us and the children.

Paul (Mediator): Dave, do you agree?

Dave: Yes, Beth is right. We're arguing a lot and the kids see it. It's not fun.

Paul (Mediator): Then it sounds to me like we need to look at the possibility of a temporary settlement agreement. That means that one of you will leave the marital home. It will be voluntary and by mutual consent, but the first decision must be who is going to leave. Have you talked this over between yourselves?

Dave: Yes, the subject's come up, but we have a problem. Beth thinks that I should be the one to leave, but I'm not the one who wants this divorce. I don't think it's right that I should have to move out of my house.

Beth: Dave knows that I have more time for the children than he has and there is no question that the kids are staying at home.

Dave: Beth is right, she does have more time for the kids, but I usually get home by 5:30. A few nights a week I might have to go to a meeting, but we've never had trouble with a babysitter before.

Beth: Now you know what the problem is! He'd rather have the children stay with a babysitter than me.

Dave: I didn't say that.

Beth: That's exactly what you said.

Paul (Mediator): Wait a minute, what I'm really interested in is what you see as best for the family. Dave, would I be correct in saying that you might feel some resentment if you were the one to leave?

Dave: Yes, that's right, I would feel resentful.

Beth: Worst of all, the kids would bear the burden of his resentment all the time.

Dave: That's not fair. I know you've been a good mother, but I've been a good father, too. I wouldn't lay my resentment on the kids.

Beth: O.K., perhaps I was too hasty, but the fact remains that I should be with the children, not a babysitter. Is a babysitter going to check their homework? No.

Dave: I would do that when I got home.

Paul (Mediator): O.K., let me ask this then. Where would each of you stay if you moved out?

Dave: I guess I'd have to take an apartment.

Beth: Why couldn't you stay with your folks for awhile? They have the room.

Dave: I could do that, but for obvious reasons, I'd rather not.

Beth: If I left, I could stay at a friend's apartment for a little while anyway. She has a den I could use.

Paul (Mediator): You know, there is a good chance we could have an agreement in about two months. That's really not such a long time and frankly, I have an idea that may work. A few times in the past, in situations like yours, the spouses actually agreed to alternate staying in the house each week. That is only while they negotiated their agreement. Never a long term arrangement. It sounds to me like the two of you are in a position to give that some thought.

Beth: It's an idea. I don't know how the kids would take it though.

Paul (Mediator): What we generally know about children who are going through their parents' divorce is that what is most important to them is that they don't feel rejected or abandoned by one of their parents. Closeness to both their parents is very important.

Dave: Well, what you are suggesting seems to make sense then. We'll both have equal time with them. Also, I might schedule my evening appointments on the weeks I'll be out of the house and when I can't do that perhaps Beth will want to spend the evening with them.

Beth: It might work. I think you're right. The kids need both of us and this seems like a fair, practical way to do it.

Paul (Mediator) : All right, tell you what. You both have to make certain that your temporary living arrangements can be handled. How about if you check that out and let's schedule another session toward the end of this week.

Beth and Dave: O.K.

See Appendix D for Beth and Dave's temporary settlement agreement.

THE PROPERTY SETTLEMENT

Property, in all its forms, is highly valued in our society. As a practical people, we clearly understand the relationship between property and how well we do or do not live. It is no wonder, therefore, that divorce cases involving property disputes can be among the most hotly and bitterly contested. Similarly, it is not surprising to find lawyers calling marital settlement agreements, "property" settlement agreements, signifying the importance we place on property in the overall scheme of things. Marital settlement agreements routinely provide for child custody, child support and spousal support, in addition to divisions and allocations of property between the spouses.

Because property is so significant to separating and divorcing spouses, this guide will devote considerable attention to the five functions provided by divorce mediation to spouses as they negotiate their property interests. Those functions are: (1) Identification of all property; (2) Identification and valuation of marital property; (3) Allocation of nonmarital property between the spouses; (4) Division of marital property between the spouses; and (5) Adjustment and division of marital debt.

Identifying All Property

Essential to a successful and fair divorce settlement is identifying all property owned by each spouse and all property in which either has an interest. Spouses who wish to mediate their divorce must be willing and prepared to disclose to the mediator and the other spouse, all such property. The mediator will spend a considerable amount of time discussing property issues with both spouses. He will also independently review all documentation relating to their property. Couples will be asked to produce two or more years' income tax returns and any financial statements provided to banks or other lending institutions during this same period. On rare occasions the mediator may indicate a need for an accountant to review the records to insure that all property has been properly identified. If the mediator and spouses agree, an impartial accountant will be retained to review the records for this purpose.

It must be emphasized, however, that the mere existence of property does not, in itself, make that property subject to division between spouses. Only "marital property" will be divided, except as the couple may otherwise agree is appropriate. Marital property was described in Chapter Two; worth repeating, however, is that marital property is all property acquired during the marriage, other than property received by gift or inheritance by one spouse only. It does not matter which spouse earned the property or in whose name the property is titled.

Spouses usually possess, or have an interest, in both marital and nonmarital property. In order to avoid conflict after the separation, couples identify both marital and nonmarital property in mediation, and agree first on how they will distribute nonmarital property between them.

As an aid to identifying your marital and nonmarital property interests, we have included a form useful for this purpose in Appendix E. In most instances, the kinds of property listed are well known and need little explanation. Some words, however, need to be said about pensions, business and professional interests, life insurance, and real estate.

Pensions

In recent years, perhaps no other employee benefit has drawn as much public attention as pensions. As the federal government has passed sweeping legislation protecting pension plans from mismanagement and bankruptcy, employers and employees have placed more and more emphasis on these plans as a means of providing long-term financial security for workers. It is rare for a divorce and separation to occur that does not involve consideration of pension rights.

We obviously cannot speak for the laws of every state, but generally, pension rights are considered marital property. (Beginning on February 1, 1983, federal law authorizes military pensions to be considered marital property to the same extent as non-military pensions under state law.) Mediation expressly recognizes the importance and fairness of including pension rights as marital property, and unless your state laws explicitly exempt pensions from marital property, pensions will be considered marital property in mediation.

Pensions, however, are unique financial creatures. They are sometimes difficult to value in present dollars, and the person who has actually earned the pension often feels a sense of unfairness in claims against it. Mediators will want the following information about pensions before discussions about them begin:

1. Is the pension vested? If not, when will the pension vest? (Vesting designates the amount of time an employee must work before the employee is entitled to participate in the pension plan.)
2. To what extent has the employee contributed directly to the pension plan from his or her earnings?
3. What is the formula for employer contributions?
4. At what future date will the pension become available to the employee?
5. Can the pension be valued in present dollars? (Provided sufficient information exists, accountants and actuaries can value many pension rights in present dollars.)
6. To what extent did the marriage exist while pension rights were accruing?

Typically, couples choose one of two ways to reach agreement concerning their pension interests. The first of these requires that the present value of the pension be known, for example, $30,000. A husband who has a pension worth $30,000 may purchase his wife's stake in the pension for an amount the couple agrees is fair. A payment plan for this purchase is also negotiated. The second method used assigns part of the pension to each spouse at the time the pension is actually paid out. Under this approach, the pension administrator is instructed to pay the pension, in proportions the couple agrees is fair, to both husband and wife, at the time the pension matures and is paid out.

Business and Professional Interests

Where one or both spouses develop their own business or professional practice during the marriage relationship, the business or practice is considered marital property, and requires evaluation. The services of an impartial accountant are normally required for this purpose. Generally, the accountant asks what the business or professional practice would bring in the open market if it were offered for sale.

Often, however, a spouse becomes highly reluctant to treat his or her business in the same way as other marital property assets. Consider the following exchange between Beth, Dave and Paul.

Paul (Mediator): Dave and Beth, it looks like we've identified and valued all your assets except Dave's business.

Dave: I can tell you, we have a problem here.

Paul (Mediator): Why, Dave?

Dave: Because I don't care what the accountant says the business is worth; I know that without me it's hardly worth anything.

Paul (Mediator): Do you mean that if it were to be put on the market for sale and you weren't going to stay in the business, the accountant's estimate of what the business is worth is wrong?

Dave: Absolutely, the business works because of my personal contacts and the trust my customers have in me. Take that away, and the business just won't be worth a fraction of what you would expect, looking at its financial records.

Beth: I'm not sure I agree. The business has good existing accounts. If the business were sold, those accounts would still be there for the next owner.

Dave: Those accounts would dry up over night. Believe me, I'm the business. Besides, if I had to buy Beth out of the business, I couldn't do it.

Beth: Well, the accountant says the business is worth $80,000. As far as I'm concerned, that's it. The business is marital property and I want my fair share.

Dave: I can't accept that. I've slaved to make that business something these last five years and without me, it's not worth $10,000. I think we have to terminate this and go to court.

Paul (Mediator): I know this is a problem and not necessarily an unusual one. I have seen spouses change an accountant's appraisal of the value of a small business for the exact reasons Dave has stated. Beth, let me ask you a question. What is it about the business that you'll be giving up after your divorce?

Beth: That's easy. The business is security.

Paul (Mediator): When you say security, do you mean future income?

Beth: Yes.

Paul (Mediator): Then I have an idea. I suggest we defer this part of our discussion about the business until we get to spousal support. We may be able to find a way to tie some portion of spousal support to the future performance of Dave's business.

Dave: I would be willing to try that. I could see giving Beth some of the future earnings from the business if it continues the way it's going. That seems fair.

Beth: Ok. I'm willing to take a look at that. I don't want Dave to have to sell the business to pay me.

Paul (Mediator) : Fine, we'll give it a try later, then.

A variation on the question of a spouse's right to some part of a business or professional practice will sometimes occur when one spouse has supported the other through school. The spouse who worked while the other attended school often feels that he or she should be compensated for his or her financial contribution toward the degree. In these situations, the mediator will try to guide the spouses into a discussion of the actual financial investment made by the spouse who worked while the other obtained a degree. Based on this information, the spouses usually are able to reach agreement on this sensitive issue.

Life Insurance

There are generally two types of life insurance, known respectively as "term" and "whole life." "Term" insurance purchases protection in the event of death, while "whole life" insurance provides death benefits and also accumulates what is known as cash value. Cash value is the amount of money available to the owner of the policy if the policy were to be discontinued. Cash value may also be borrowed against at low interest rates. The cash value of whole life insurance is marital property and is easily determined. Usually a phone call to the company or its local agent obtains the desired information. Term insurance is not considered marital property.

Real Estate and The Family Home

Real estate is often the single largest marital property asset owned by a couple and presents its own set of issues which need to be explored and resolved in mediation. Again, all real estate owned by each spouse must be identified and valued. Typically, real estate appraisers are retained to perform this service. The value of real property is determined by the appraiser after he or she has carefully reviewed the sale prices of similar properties in the neighborhood within the recent past. Couples are presented with an appraisal report which states these findings.

It is important to note that it is equity value that is significant to a separating couple, not the total value of their real estate. Equitable value is the total worth of the real estate, less the amount of the outstanding mortgage, other obligations and the cost of selling the property.

It is not unusual for the family home, which of course is real property, to occupy a particular place of importance in divorce negotiations. Often, the family home is the single most valuable item of marital property. Sometimes, it assumes significant personal importance to one or both spouses because of efforts made over the years to improve the home. Where the couple has young children, there is enormous reluctance to do anything which will displace the children from their normal environment. Finally, on occasion, custody disputes become improperly linked to the question of which parent will retain the marital home.

Skilled mediators very carefully sift through these highly charged emotional and practical considerations with the spouses. It is impossible here, of course, to detail all of the possible results of such negotiations. One option which has been helpful when emotional issues are linked to the marital home is to agree upon how equity will be divided when the home is sold, but to delay the actual sale.

A point should also be made concerning the tax consequences of a sale of the marital home. Capital gains taxes may have to be paid (depending on the amount of appreciation of the home during ownership) if the marital home is sold to a third party, with profits being divided between husband and wife. If either spouse purchases the other's interest in the home, capital gains taxes may also have to be paid. Couples should know, however, of the following tax rules which may be helpful in minimizing capital gains taxes in these circumstances.

The first rule provides that where a spouse has realized a capital gain (or profit) on the sale of a residence, then any such gain may be reinvested in another place of residence within twenty-four (24) months, and no tax is due. The second rule provides that if a spouse is fifty-five (55) or older, and has lived in a house for three of the last five years, a one-time capital gain exemption of up to one hundred twenty-five thousand dollars ($125,000.00) may exist. Often an accountant is asked to provide the precise exemption amounts for each spouse.

Premarital Assets

Premarital assets are property brought into a marriage by one or both spouses. Premarital assets are not marital property, but are sometimes difficult to identify and value because such assets are often commingled with marital assets. Similarly, it is not unusual for a number of years to have passed since the spouses had premarital assets, and records and memories may be vague at the present time.

Under these circumstances, the spouses and the mediator explore the property of the spouses before marriage as carefully as possible, and try to best estimate the respective property worth of each spouse at the time of marriage. If the separate spousal assets were essentially equal in value, then, of course, no problem exists. If a disparity of assets did exist at the time of marriage, then the parties need to come to agreement about the size of the disparity. Based on what the parties believe is fair, a credit may be given to the marriage partner who had the larger of the premarital assets.

An example of this situation may be useful. Carol and Jim were married in 1973. At the time of the marriage, Jim had his own fully paid new automobile, purchased for Three Thousand Five Hundred ($3,500) Dollars. He also owned Sixty-Five (65) shares of stock, worth approximately Four Thousand ($4,000) Dollars. Carol had Fifteen Hundred ($1,500) Dollars in a savings account, which was immediately used to purchase furniture. Jim's stock was sold sometime around 1976, and the proceeds were used to buy more stock held in both Carol and Jim's names. Jim's automobile was traded-in in 1977 for the automobile that Carol has been driving for the last five years.

Under these circumstances, the fair value of Jim's car is estimated as of the date of marriage. In this case, the estimate is Two Thousand, Eight Hundred ($2,800) Dollars (once a car is driven there is an immediate depreciation, hence $2,800, not $3,500). Jim's premarital assets were worth Six Thousand Eight Hundred ($6,800) Dollars and Carol's premarital assets were worth Fifteen Hundred ($1,500) Dollars. Carol and Jim are selling their home and expect a significant profit. They want premarital assets to be calculated into their respective shares of the profits. Therefore, Jim will receive $5,300 more from the sale of the house than Carol.

Family Gifts

When a couple is married, it is customary for them to receive gifts of money or property from friends and family. Normally, at the time of separation, no problem arises regarding such gifts, except where a fairly substantial gift was made by the family of one of the spouses. Should both spouses share in a division of the gift at the time of separation? The spouse whose family made the gift claims that it was not made in contemplation of divorce, while the other spouse claims that it was a gift for the couple to share. The circumstances of each case need to be reviewed carefully, but, generally, gifts made under these circumstances are considered gifts to the marriage relationship in which each spouse has an interest. Couples are usually able to arrive at a fair division of such gifts through mediation.

Active Versus Passive Growth of Nonmarital Property

Sometimes nonmarital property has increased in value because of the active work of one or both of the spouses during the marriage relationship. Where this has occurred, the spouses need to reach agreement on the amount of such increase and include that increase as marital property for later division. For example, let us say that Carol had $10,000 in a bank account at the beginning of her marital relationship to Jim. Over the years, the money was left alone, and collected interest. At the time of separation, $15,000 is in the bank. Through no effort of the spouses, this nonmarital property grew in value by $5,000. In this circumstance, the full $15,000 is still considered nonmarital property because the increase in value occurred through passive ownership.

On the other hand, let us take the same $10,000 of nonmarital property, and this time, instead of being placed in the bank, it was used to purchase a rental house. The house was rented and produced rental income during the marriage relationship. The work of maintaining the house and collecting the rent was shared between the spouses. At the time of separation, the rental house had an equitable value of $25,000. Clearly, $10,000 of the present value in the rental property is considered nonmarital property and belongs to the spouse who had the $10,000 at the time the marriage began. However, the $15,000 value increase is marital property because active participation of the spouses was a factor in producing the increase in property value. When this situation occurs, the spouses need to carefully review the circumstances surrounding such value increases and arrive at an agreement as to what portion of the increase is marital property, and how it can be fairly divided.

Nonmarital Property and Household Effects

After a couple has identified all property and has agreed which is marital property and which is nonmarital property, it is ordinarily a very easy matter to divide the nonmarital property between the spouses. Care should be taken, however, to carefully set forth the nonmarital property in writing and to identify, in each case, to whom it belongs. This list is often attached to the marital settlement agreement in order to insure that future disputes are avoided.

It is also suggested that household effects (furniture, silver, etc.) and automobiles be divided up at this time, in effect treating such items as a separate class of marital property. The reasons for this approach are first, the spouses usually have clear preferences as to which property they want to take with them, and second, the spouses are usually able to work out a fair division of this property between themselves without the help of the mediator. Finally, reaching agreement on a division of the household effects and automobiles helps to establish a proper tone for further negotiations concerning division of marital property.

Division of Marital Property

Once all marital property has been identified and valued, and the nonmarital property and household effects have been divided, the couple's last task is to divide the remaining marital property. The actual division can occur in several different ways, and we will turn to those momentarily. Before property division, however, an orderly and logical process must be established which will insure a fair division of the property. In order to do this, it is suggested that the spouses and mediator focus their attention first on total property value (that is, arrive at a total dollar amount which the property is worth at the present time).

Again, joining Beth and Dave Malone, we will assume they have marital property worth One Hundred Thousand ($100,000) Dollars; Forty Thousand ($40,000) Dollars is equitable value in the marital home; Ten Thousand ($10,000) Dollars is pension value and Fifty Thousand ($50,000) Dollars consists of cash on hand, stocks, and cash value on a whole life insurance policy. We will further assume, for the purposes of this example, that Beth and Dave have decided to sell the marital home. They expect to have One Hundred Thousand ($100,000) Dollars of marital property to divide between themselves.

Beth and Dave now reach that point in their negotiations where they are discussing how the $100,000 should be divided between them. The following is, of course, a condensed version of a mediation dialogue.

Paul (Mediator): Beth and Dave, you have made enormous progress up to this point. I think that it would be worth pointing out that you have reached agreement in a number of areas. First, you agreed to mediate your marriage termination. Secondly, you reached agreement on the terms of a temporary separation. Finally, you have now agreed on the total amount of the marital property to be divided, except for Dave's business, which we are deferring until we talk about spousal support. Our next task is to find a fair and equitable division between you of your marital property.

Beth: I'm very concerned here. Dave made practically all our money while we were married, and the $100,000, well, it's all money he made. But I feel I have a right to a fair part of it.

Paul (Mediator): Beth, why do you feel you have a right to this property?

Beth: I know that I was essentially a housewife during our marriage, but what I did allowed Dave to have a nice house to live in, eat well, and two great kids. I worked hard, too.

Paul (Mediator): Are you saying that without your help, Dave couldn't have had all those things and a career as well?

Beth: Yes.

Paul (Mediator): Dave, how do Beth's feelings sound to you?

Dave: I realize how she feels, but I think she's forgotten something. Before we got married, she had a teaching career, but she decided to get married. I promised to support her, not give her half of every dime I make. Well, I supported her, and now it's over. Maybe she should go out and make enough money to save $100,000.

Paul (Mediator): Yes, I understand why you might feel a strong attachment to the family savings, but I heard you say two things that strike me. First, you said you understand how Beth feels, and second, you said you didn't promise when you were married to give her one-half of every dime you made. That sounds to me like you think Beth has some right to the family savings, but not 50%. Is that right?

Dave: Sure, she's entitled to something, but remember, I'm going to be paying support too, for a while. I can't work for her for the rest of my life. Also, I really feel strongly about my pension. I won't even be seeing that money for years, and I've got to pay her for it now. Also, I worked awfully hard for that pension.

Beth: I understand how Dave feels about his pension, but this business about working for me the rest of his life is a lot of bunk. Other than the pension, the $100,000 is there to be divided up. He won't be working to pay for that.

Dave: No, you're right, I already worked for it all.

Paul (Mediator) : All right, at some point in our discussions about property, I usually say this, "OK, I want you to assume that the basic rule in property division of family savings is 50-50. Now, each of you tell me why it should be different." In your case, I've already heard why you think it should be different.

Beth: I never said it should be different.

Paul (Mediator) : Yes, I think you did when you said you understand how Dave felt about his pension.

Beth: Oh, Ok, yes, I understand how he feels about his pension, and it's true, he won't be getting it for a while, but other than the pension, I think I would be entitled to 50% of the property. Unless I did what I did, Dave couldn't have made it.

Paul (Mediator) : It appears, Dave, that an offer has been placed on the table. Does it seem fair to you?

Dave: Fifty percent, other than my pension?

Paul (Mediator) : Beth, is that correct?

Beth: Yes.

Dave: Forty-five Thousand Dollars?

Paul (Mediator) : It looks that way.

Dave: It hurts, but it seems fair. Ok.

    This exchange illustrates several important points concerning mediation, but perhaps none so significant as the value of creating a settlement context in which the spouses have an opportunity to hear the legitimate concerns and views of one another and to react to those concerns and views. In this particular exchange, Beth was given a chance to express why she felt her role as a housewife entitled her to a fair share of the marital property, and Dave had an opportunity to explain why he felt his pension was something that should be treated separately. Invariably, when the spouses in divorce mediation approach discussions in this manner, agreement is reached. Contrast this approach to adversarial divorce where the spouses are normally instructed by their lawyers not to talk to one another and are never given a chance to cooperatively settle matters between themselves directly.

    Another significant point made in Beth and Dave's dialogue concerns the basic approach mediation takes to property division. Specifically, the spouses begin their discussions on the assumption that they each have an equal interest in the marital property, and then explain or try to explain why that would not be fair. Each situation is unique.

How would a division of property between Beth and Dave have been influenced if either of them had significant property independent of the marital property? Or if one had a business that would go bankrupt because of a sudden reduction in personal worth? The questions are endless and we are not here attempting to create neat formulas for every conceivable circumstance. Rather, our purpose is to demonstrate the cooperative nature of mediation and to express the view that mediation provides a divorce settlement context which maximizes the spouse's abilities to have their own legitimate needs met.

It is also worth noting how the mediator interacted with Beth and Dave during their exchange. The mediator never became a bargainer or negotiator for either of them; rather, the mediator intervened to permit each spouse to express his views and to keep the discussion moving. Proficient mediators never impose or try to impose their values on the spouses, but rather strive to create bargaining conditions, within the mediation context, in which the spouses fairly arrive at mutually acceptable solutions to their separation and divorce problems.

Methods of Dividing Marital Property

After the spouses have agreed on the proportionate division of marital property between them, their next task is to design a plan to accomplish the division. In the previous example, the easiest set of circumstances existed with which to design such a plan. This was so because all of the marital property was either in liquid asset form (cash), or could be readily put in such form. In many situations, however, such circumstances do not exist. The most common reasons which prevent an immediate and full division of marital property relate to the marital home and the business or professional interests of one or both spouses.

The marital home is often retained by one spouse on a permanent basis. It is not unusual for that spouse to purchase the other's interest in the home over a period of time. Such arrangements must be carefully worked out and consideration should be given to such matters as interest on the purchase amount and when the actual transfer of legal title will occur. When one spouse has an interest in the business or professional practice of the other, normally a long term payout of that interest is arranged. Again, care must be taken to provide the terms of the reimbursement.

It is usually not difficult to devise a plan for the actual division of marital property. Mediators are particularly helpful in this area because of their ability, based on experience, to suggest the various available options and alternatives for such a plan.

Marital Debt

Marriage partners usually accumulate some marital debt during their marriage relationship, and needless to say, the issues raised by the separation, as they relate to marital debt, must be discussed in mediation.

There are typically three types of marital debt: (1) Debt arising from revolving charge accounts; (2) Debt arising from retail installment loans; and (2) Mortgage debt.

Each type of debt is somewhat different from the other and requires specifically-tailored treatment.

Revolving charge accounts with banks and department stores are extremely common and are easily identified by the charge cards most of us carry. The balances on each of these accounts, as of the date of separation, must be identified. The spouses then determine their respective responsibilities for repayment of these debts after separation. In addition, the banks or stores extending the charge cards must be notified of the separation in order that joint accounts be closed and new individual accounts be opened, assuming the credit worthiness of each spouse will permit the establishment of individual credit. Our experience suggests that revolving charge creditors are most willing to work with a separating couple to establish new accounts and even allocate previous balances between the new accounts to avoid the need for a total payoff of the existing account at the time of separation.

A further consideration regarding revolving charge accounts concerns the ability of wives to open accounts in their own names. One of the ways this can be accomplished is for the husband to agree to be a guarantor for a specified and limited period of time and amount, while the wife has an opportunity to establish her own credit history. Mediation permits the spouses to explore such alternatives, which typically would not be available, or even considered, in adversarial divorce.

The second type of marital debt relates to what is known as a retail credit account. This type of debt is typically entered into by marriage partners when they jointly purchase large household related items such as furniture and appliances. Automobile loans, when they are made directly with automobile dealers, also are included in this category. This type of loan involves signing a purchase contract and related documents which stipulate, among other information, the amount of the loan, the number of monthly payments and the amount of each payment. Unlike revolving charge accounts, these loans are not subject to change, according to new purchases, on a monthly basis. Also, unlike revolving charge accounts, these loans will remain a joint obligation, from the creditors' point of view, after separation and divorce. The goal in mediation is to allocate responsibility for the repayment of these loans over their remaining life. Normally, one spouse or the other will assume full responsibility for the loan repayment. Under these circumstances, the marital settlement agreement will provide for such responsibility and will protect the spouse who is not responsible for the loan repayment.

The final common type of marital debt relates to mortgage loans on real property which are customarily joint obligations of husband and wife. If the real property is to be sold upon separation, problems relating to this debt are eliminated because the proceeds from the sale will be used to retire the debt. In other instances, however, mortgage debt must be reviewed quite carefully. Spouses should also be aware of a provision which may exist in their mortgage which permits lenders to accelerate repayment of the debt, if the spouses are divorced. If such a mortgage provision does exist, then appropriate discussions in mediation need to address this issue.

Generally, marital debts do not create significant problems to divorcing couples, and where the spouses are fully prepared to discuss such matters in the context of mediation, agreement is typically reached.

Finally...

If you read the preceding pages about property straight through, as you might read a novel, we suspect that divorce may not be in the offing for you. You are probably tempted to say: NOTHING IS WORTH THAT!

At first, the subject of property may seem complex and even overwhelming. It does not have to be. First, remember that we described a broad spectrum of property concerns and many of them may not apply to you. Second, the mediator is the expert in this area, not you! The mediator's job is to guide you through a detailed review of your property interests and to carefully explain property matters to you so that you will not be confused. In our experience, property negotiations have been most successful when the mediator is able to help both spouses understand all of their property issues. The mediator, therefore, has this objective as a first priority.

We also urge you to carefully review Appendix E (Financial Information and Income Statement). You should realize that when you and your spouse complete this form, you have created the foundation for your negotiations. Everything we have said in this Chapter relates to this financial information form in one fashion or another. Completing and understanding this form will not only serve your negotiations well, but will also be a meaningful educational experience that will help make your future financial planning easier and more organized.

In conclusion, do not think that only attorneys are able to understand and make appropriate decisions about your property interests. In fact, we have found that spouses who negotiate their own property interests will often be more sensitive to important issues and concerns than an attorney would be. This is because you, and not your attorney, are the person directly involved in those issues and concerns. Understanding and negotiating property issues is not only within your capability, but it probably cannot be done better by anyone else.

FINANCIAL SUPPORT

The flexibility a couple has in choosing a spousal support plan that suits their specific needs can be seen in the following clauses taken from legal settlement agreements.

Husband shall pay to Wife the sum of $500 per month, permanent, nonmodifiable alimony, on the first day of each month following the signing of this marital settlement agreement until the first to occur of the following:
- (1) Wife's remarriage or
- (2) The death of Husband or Wife.

Husband and Wife are each gainfully employed and expect to remain so. Spousal support or alimony is not claimed by either from the other, and Husband and Wife waive alimony or spousal support, past, present and future.

Husband shall pay to Wife the sum of $500 per month for 24 months or until the first to occur of the following:
- (1) Wife's remarriage or
- (2) The death of Husband or Wife.

Two years from the date this marital settlement agreement is signed, the parties shall return to mediation for the purpose of reviewing their respective financial conditions and determining the further status of spousal support. Wife shall make every reasonable effort to become economically independent during the 24 months the spousal support is to be paid as provided for herein.

What we must emphasize is that spousal support, in mediation, is not determined through a legal power struggle in which each spouse fights bitterly for all he or she can get. Rather, it is based on the legitimate needs and resources which each spouse will have after their separation.

Typically, spousal support is not discussed until a couple has reached agreement on their property settlement. This is a logical sequence because the property settlement goes far in helping a couple clarify what their actual resources will be once they have separated; it also defines the financial obligations each spouse will have.

The Budget Review

Essential to negotiations about spousal support is the budget review. The primary purpose of this review is to help spouses understand what their respective day to day financial needs will be after their separation (see Appendix F for Monthly Expense Budget Form). Another purpose of the review is to help the spouses identify and eliminate or reduce unnecessary expense. A good example of this recently occurred when during the course of mediation, the subject of life insurance premiums came up. This couple was very interested in protecting their children if something should happen to the father, but the budget review revealed that the monthly premium payments were too high. It turned out that all of the couple's life insurance was of the whole life variety and that the same protection could be obtained by converting at least some of the insurance to term protection, at far reduced costs.

The combination of the property settlement and the budget review provides a couple with the hard data they need to make intelligent decisions about spousal support. Furthermore, decisions about spousal support are often preceded by discussions as to how income may be increased by one or both spouses. For instance, is the wife able and willing to return to school to increase her job related skills? If so, what expenses will be incurred if she does return to school? Answers to these questions are extremely important.

Designing an appropriate plan for spousal support may include conditions when spousal support payments are to be increased or decreased. For example, a couple may agree that if the wife returns to school to obtain or increase job related skills, support payments will be increased to help pay for tuition. Conversely, the agreement may provide a formula whereby support payments are decreased when the wife obtains employment. For instance, this formula may provide for a reduction in spousal support of fifty cents for every take home dollar earned by the wife. Such an approach encourages the wife's independence by increasing her income while providing the husband with reduced support payments. Otherwise, the wife's starting salary might result in an income that would be less than what she was receiving in alimony, a situation which would deprive her of financial incentive.

It should be apparent that mediation provides couples with enormous flexibility to design a fair support plan. Such flexibility is rarely, if ever, achieved in adversarial divorce.

Health Insurance

In considering spousal support, a special word must be said about health insurance. It is not unusual for this important benefit to be provided to an entire family through a group insurance plan at the husband's place of employment. A wife can normally continue to be covered under such a plan until the divorce becomes final. Legal separation does not, as a general rule, remove a wife's coverage. Also, minor children are always entitled to coverage regardless of custody arrangements.

After a divorce becomes final, however, a wife should be prepared to obtain her own health insurance. This may influence her future budget and the couple's future support planning.

The Support Negotiations

Beth and Dave have now reached that point in their discussions where the issue of spousal support is being negotiated. You will recall that Beth and Dave deferred the question of Beth's interest in Dave's business for now.

Paul (Mediator): Beth and Dave, it is clear from your budget review that Beth is going to need some help making ends meet, at least for a while. The situation should improve when Beth obtains a full time job, but that clearly isn't going to happen overnight. Also, I don't want either of you to think that I've forgotten our discussions about Beth's interest in Dave's business.

Dave: Oh, I wasn't the least concerned that we would forget that point.

Paul (Mediator): Now, the way it looks is that Beth will have net income for the time being of $125 per week for at least eight months. Hopefully, by the start of next year's school term, that will change.

Dave: Those income estimates, though, don't include any interest Beth will be earning on the money she will get from our division of property. Remember, Beth will have $45,000 in cash to invest.

Beth: First of all, I have no idea what interest I can get on that money. More importantly, though, I feel that that money is my savings. Before, my savings was in a house that appreciated each year. I think that I am entitled to keep getting interest on that money that I don't have to use to pay my rent.

Dave: You know, Beth, that just isn't fair. I know that I am going to have to dip into my savings to keep things going at least for a while, probably, until you get a full time job.

Paul (Mediator): Perhaps, I can be helpful here. We know that the process of separation usually means a reduction in the standard of living of both husband and wife, normally for some period of time. It is something neither likes, of course, but it is a reality that must be confronted. Fortunately, the reduction is often for a temporary period of time. It is helpful when both the husband and wife recognize that to be the case, and are willing to fairly share the burden. In your case, you will each have substantial resources to draw on and I suggest you do so fairly.

Beth: That sounds reasonable, and it does look like Dave will have to go into his savings for a while. I don't know how much it will help, but I agree to use the interest from the $45,000 to pay my expenses.

Paul (Mediator): Beth, I think that you have just given yourself a good homework assignment. What you need to do is find out how that money can be invested and what kind of monthly interest will be available.

Dave: I guess there wouldn't be any harm in my doing some research also.

Paul (Mediator): Of course not. One point, though, I suggest you only look at investment opportunities that are insured. Your home was insured and this money needs to be treated the same way. Any problems?

Beth and Dave: No.

Paul (Mediator): Should we tackle the question of Beth's interest in Dave's business now or wait until our next session?

Dave: No, wait, I have been doing a lot of thinking about that and I have a proposal to make.

Paul (Mediator): Let's hear it. Beth, you agree?

Beth: I wouldn't miss it for the world.

Paul (Mediator): You have our attention.

Dave: First, I recognize that Beth does have a legitimate interest in my business. She paid for the tuition on my Master's degree, she helped in the office for the first couple of years, and we spent about $20,000 in our savings to get my business off the ground.

Beth: Thank you for recognizing those things.

Dave: Now, the accountant says that the business is worth $80,000. I disagree with that, as I said earlier, but for the moment I will accept his figures and an interest in the business by Beth of $40,000. Now, here's what I propose. If Beth is willing to accept $1,000 a month which will be tax deductible alimony for me, then I will pay her $1,000 per month until the entire $40,000 is paid.

Beth: Do you mean $1,000 a month total or $1,000 a month in addition to anything else we agree to?

Dave: I mean $1,000 a month over and above anything else that is fair.

Paul (Mediator): I have two comments. First of all, I'm sure we will have to consult an accountant about how we could do that and meet I.R.S. approval, and secondly, I think Beth needs a week to consider the proposal. Do you agree, Beth?

Beth: Yes, I think I do need some time to think about that one.

Child Support

Child support is often a part of divorce negotiations. Once a decision is made about where a child will be living and with whom, it is not uncommon for the other spouse to contribute monetarily to the child's support. We emphasize, however, that both parents have a responsibility to contribute to their child's support, according to their respective resources. Mediation approaches child support in this manner.

On the monthly expense budget found in Appendix F, you will see a column on the far right side marked "Children." The purpose of this column is to help couples and their mediators identify the amount of money needed each month for child support. With this information, spouses are then able to negotiate their respective contributions.

Readers should also know that child support, like custody, is an issue that can always be raised before the courts. No agreement in these areas will prevent a court from imposing its own determinations, if asked to do so by one of the spouses. Mediation's purpose, of course, is to prevent such courtroom proceedings. This is accomplished, in regard to child support, by having the spouses arrive at fair and appropriate child support agreements in which they both have confidence. Then, if circumstances do change, mediation, instead of the courts, is available to help the spouses reach new agreements.

Couples should also know that a major problem related to divorce in this country is the collection of child support by one spouse from the other, where the support payments have been ordered by a divorce court. Millions of dollars each year are not paid and spouses are spending large sums of money on attorney's fees to collect these unpaid support obligations, often without success. Recent research has clearly shown that mediated divorce settlements are being adhered to much more rigorously than court imposed settlements.[1] It therefore seems much more likely that child support payments will be made regularly and on time when such payments are agreed to through mediated negotiations rather than ordered by the courts.

Often, the last issue to be negotiated relates to future college education expenses and specifically, who will be responsible, if anyone, to pay such costs. The legal obligation to support a child terminates upon the child's reaching the age of majority, usually 18 years of age. Paying college education expenses is, therefore, not a legal obligation which parents have. Often, however, because we value higher education so greatly, spouses want to insure that college funds will be available for children. Discussions in mediation about this issue often include consideration of who will be responsible for future college costs, or if both spouses will be responsible, how they will share the expense. Further, spouses sometimes state the limit of their future obligations to avoid being responsible for enormous college costs when there is no guarantee that money will be available to pay such costs.

In conclusion, mediation serves couples well as they negotiate spousal and child support issues. Spouses develop a firm understanding of what their resources and needs will be, as well as their children's needs, and then develop a fair support plan which best meets all of those needs without overextending available resources.

CHILDREN AND CUSTODY

This year, the lives of over one million children will be touched by divorce. These children will undergo a deep sense of loss and experience feelings of great sadness and distress resulting from the divorce process. Although most children will eventually adjust, many of them will develop emotional and behavioral problems. As a society, little has been done to reduce the effects of divorce on children. In fact, quite the opposite is true.

As a society, we have condoned the courtroom battles in which parents fight each other for custody, despite the fact that these battles are intensely destructive to the emotional well being of the children involved. The fact that children suffer from these battles is not in dispute. Research has shown us that children often respond to parental separation with a variety of symptoms: depression, regression to behavior they exhibited years before, school failure, stomach aches, headaches, delinquency.[1] Custody battles magnify and prolong these effects. Indeed, parents are often aware of the destructive consequences of adversarial divorce, but they believe that they must fight for custody and are at a loss as to what they can do to protect their children from the consequences. Unfortunately, we still continue to be improperly influenced by two deeply-seated, but recently discredited notions. The first faulty belief is that children of divorced parents can only be psychologically attached to one parent or the other, but not both. The second illogical, but long-held belief is that mothers are more fit for parenting than fathers. These beliefs encourage custody battles.

Just now, society is beginning to emerge from the dark ages of custody conflict. We do so on the basis of strong evidence gleaned from scientific studies.[2] Although controversy continues, research has clearly demonstrated that psychologically, children are best served when:

1. Close, consistent contact between a child and both parents is maintained;
2. Both parents participate meaningfully in their children's upbringing; and
3. Conflict between parents is minimized or eliminated.

These same studies have also demonstrated the following two points:

1. Children tenaciously continue to love the noncustodial parent in spite of long separations from that parent; and
2. A deep sense of loss is felt by both children and the noncustodial parent, when sole custody is awarded.

Divorce mediation undoubtedly creates an atmosphere in which these findings can be recognized, respected and utilized by parents as they attempt to redefine their relationships to their children. Mediation clearly reduces the conflict that is otherwise present in adversarial divorce. It also reduces the traumatic period of time between the child's first recognition that his or her family is being torn apart and the moment when he or she can begin to see how it will be put back together again; that reassuring moment comes only when custody agreements are clear, living arrangements are established and the child can begin to predict his future.

From Sole Custody to Joint Custody—
The Evolution Continues

Many of us have been conditioned to think that mothers are better able to nurture and support children than fathers. Judges have also been taught to presume this, and, therefore, in nine out of ten cases, they award sole custody to mothers.[3] However, history has not always viewed the mother as the superior parent in custody disputes.

Ironically, eighteenth and nineteenth century jurists were as adamant about the proper awarding of custody as twentieth century jurists, but their decisions were in the opposite direction. In the 1700's, under English common law, the father's right to custody was unquestioned. It was reasoned that because fathers were solely responsible for the financial support of their offspring, they should automatically be granted custody. During this period, even nursing infants were awarded to their fathers.

A gradual shift occurred during the 1800's, such that children were increasingly awarded to mothers. By the 1900's, children were awarded to their mothers as automatically as they had been awarded to their fathers earlier. This new maternal preference was expressed by a judge in 1938, who said, "There is but a twilight zone between mother's love and the atmosphere of heaven, and no child should be deprived of that maternal influence."[4]

In recent years, however, both state legislatures and the courts have begun to replace the maternal preference doctrine with the concept that neither parent is the presumed best parent and that parents of both sexes are equally able to raise children. For example, a Maryland statute states, "The father and mother are natural guardians and shall have equal powers and duties."[5] Similarly, in 1973, Judge Sybil Hart Kooper of New York awarded three children to their father even though the mother was not considered unfit. Judge Kooper stated that "studies of maternal deprivation have shown that the essential experience for the child is that of mothering—the warmth, consistency and continuity of the relationship, not the sex of the person who is performing the mothering function."[6]

Historically, then, custody has evolved from the notion that a father is the preferred custodial parent to the notion that a mother is the preferred custodial parent, to a preference for neither parent, but rather an award of custody based on what is in the child's best interests. Unfortunately, old habits die hard. Judges continue to predominantly award full and sole custody to mothers, effectively removing fathers from their parental rights and responsibilities. Lawyers, aware of this tendency, sometimes counsel their female clients to use this leverage specifically in an attempt to extract more money from their husbands. When this happens, children can be caught in the battlefire between their parents.

To avoid such conflicts, more and more parents are choosing joint legal custody. Both parents agree to be responsible for the major decisions affecting their child's upbringing and to cooperate about these matters in the future. Further, both parents retain a right of access to their child's health and school records. Typically, parents also agree that should any future dispute concerning their child arise, then the parents will work with a mediator to resolve the dispute prior to taking court action. Finally, joint custody obligates the parents to tell each other of any impending household move, in advance, so that new custody arrangements may be made if appropriate.

The fact that parents agree to joint legal custody does not necessarily affect the physical custody arrangements of a child. Physical custody concerns where a child lives and who is responsible for the day to day decisions affecting the child. It is not uncommon for parents to choose joint legal custody while designating one or the other of them as the physical custodial parent. Visitation arrangements are also agreed upon and described in the agreement.

The Custody Negotiations

Beth and Dave have now reached agreement on all matters relating to their separation and divorce except on the question of custody. Beth has previously heard of the maternal preference doctrine, and because of the continuing fear about her own well-being if she does not have custody, Beth has decided to "fight" for custody.

Dave has feared this point in the negotiations since mediation began. He knew custody would be a problem. Dave is confident that he is able to nurture his children as well as Beth, but he has also heard of the maternal preference doctrine. He is adamant that he does not want to be the "visiting" parent, and that he has as much right to participate in the upbringing of Chris and Billy as Beth does. At the beginning of the custody session, Dave is feeling angry and afraid.

Paul (Mediator): Dave, Beth, I want you to know how well I think you have handled your negotiations so far. Do either of you feel a sense of accomplishment up to this point?

Dave: So far, that is true, at least for me. I think we are in for a major setback today, though.

Paul (Mediator): Understandably, you are both concerned about custody. Particularly so, since it is clear to me that you each love Chris and Billy very much.

Dave: I think what it boils down to is that neither of us wants to be the "visiting" parent.

Paul (Mediator): Ok, let's look at the flip side of that statement and let me ask you this: Instead of saying what you don't want to happen as parents, tell me what it is that each of you does want as a parent.

Beth: I want regular contact with my children and I want them close to me.

Dave: I also want regular contact with them, but I also want a say in how they are raised, and I want them to know that I have a say.

Beth: Of course, I want that as well.

Paul (Mediator): It sounds to me like you both want the same things.

Beth: But that's not the way it works, is it? One or the other of us gets custody.

Paul (Mediator): I don't want to answer that just yet. Right now I'd like to look at the kinds of responsibilities that you, as parents, have toward your children.

Dave: What do you mean by "kinds" of responsibilities?

Paul (Mediator): Think about it a minute. Are there some decisions which parents are called upon to make about their children that are clearly more significant than other decisions?

Beth: Yes, I see that. Things like health and education. I think that they are more significant than whether a child goes to school with a cold.

Dave: Yes, I see that, and religious training as well.

Paul (Mediator): Do you think it would be possible for you two to cooperate in the future about the more significant decisions which you, as parents, would have to make? If you could, you might consider joint legal custody.

Dave: By cooperate, do you mean to talk to each other often?

Paul (Mediator): Well, I don't know what you mean by often, but it certainly includes the two of you talking on a regular basis about your children's well being and both participating in making the more significant decisions affecting their lives.

Beth: What if we disagree, aren't we opening ourselves up to more fighting?

Paul (Mediator): Possibly. However, we typically include a provision in marital settlement agreements that if parents disagree about such decisions, they will seek out the services of a professional counselor or mediator to help them. This seems to work very well.

Dave: All this is well and good, assuming we can cooperate, but it doesn't tell us where the kids will live.

Paul (Mediator): Right, and we're coming to that. All I would like to know now is whether the two of you think you can cooperate in the future about your children, regardless of where they live on a day-to-day basis. What do you each think about that?

Dave: I think that's a tall order.

Paul (Mediator): Let's talk about cooperation a moment. During our work these recent weeks, has either of you felt that you were actually trying to cooperate with the other?

Beth: Yes, and you know it's funny you should ask that. I think it was just yesterday that I thought about the same thing.

Paul (Mediator): Beth, tell us how you felt you were trying to cooperate with Dave these recent weeks.

Beth: Ok, I'll try. After about our second meeting with you, I realized that if I wanted something, I needed to give something back. And every time I gave something back, what I got was worth more than what I gave up. Pretty soon, I started looking for things to give up, so that I could get what I wanted. Sometimes I thought Dave was doing it too.

Paul (Mediator): How does that strike you, Dave?

Dave: I know what Beth is saying. I noticed the same thing.

Paul (Mediator): Well, don't you each think you can continue to deal this way with one another in the future about your children and other things as they come up?

Dave: I don't know. I think what we've done in this room is possible because you're here.

Paul (Mediator): I'm not sure about that. I know that the two of you have talked about some things without me.

Dave: That's true. Still...

Paul (Mediator): You see, what's really important here is your children. Solid research shows clearly that kids will continue to love both their parents after divorce and will thrive best when they know each of you participates in their upbringing.

Beth: I really don't think we have any choice. We need to cooperate for Chris and Billy. I'm certainly willing to try.

Dave: Yes, me too. It makes sense. Ok, then regardless of where Chris and Billy actually live, Beth and I will cooperate about their upbringing and in case of disagreement, we will agree to work with a counselor or mediator to help us reach decisions. Yes, I'll agree to that. Still, where will our children live?

Paul (Mediator): Ok, that takes care of legal custody. The next point is physical custody and the extent that you can practically share physical custody, with one proviso.

Beth: Which is?

Paul (Mediator): The courts like to know that one of you is the parent who has final authority on those day-to-day decisions we talked about earlier. The courts want to know that parents won't be running into court every time they disagree about such things.

Beth: So, what you're really saying is that one of us will have physical custody?

Paul (Mediator): Yes, final responsibility on those type of day-to-day decisions. Usually, we ask where the children will be spending most of their time and designate that parent as the physical custodial parent.

Dave: You said most of their time. Does that mean they can actually stay with both of us?

Paul (Mediator): Probably, but that depends on a lot of things, such as schools, friends, and your respective availabilities to them during their non-school time. There are of course other things to consider as well.

Beth: Can we have joint legal custody, even if we don't share physical custodial arrangements?

Paul (Mediator): Absolutely, but let me emphasize that regardless of whether or not you can share physical custody, we'll still discuss how you can each maximize your time with your children. Let me ask you each this. Do you think that these kinds of arrangements will work for you?

Beth: I think it's worth giving it a good try.

Dave: I think so too. In fact, I have an idea. I think Beth and I may be able to agree on the physical custody arrangements of Chris and Billy between ourselves. I'd like to try.

Paul (Mediator) : Sounds good to me. Beth?

Beth: Sure.

Paul (Mediator) : Ok, good. I think you've made some very helpful decisions today, both for yourselves and your children. I'll expect to hear from you about the physical custody matters, say, by the end of next week.

TAXES AND DIVORCE

The purpose of this chapter is to help you understand the tax consequences of your separation and divorce. Hopefully, this understanding will lead to intelligent negotiation between you and your spouse about relevant tax matters. Tax issues, like all others discussed in mediation, are best resolved after both spouses fully understand the options which are available to them. Only then can they appropriately trade various advantages and disadvantages, (if any), between them.

The best way to approach taxes is to look at each of the component parts of a divorce settlement and then describe the possible tax effects on each. Again, it is not our intention that you become tax experts. Taxes are complicated, the laws change, and the situations vary. Your mediator and tax advisers should be consulted before reaching any final agreements.

THE PROPERTY SETTLEMENT
Capital Gains

When we refer to the property settlement we are discussing the various decisions made concerning marital property: specifically, how that property is being distributed between the spouses and whether any titling changes will be required.

Prior to the tax changes which occurred in 1984, if one spouse had an interest in property and transferred that interest to the other spouse as part of the divorce settlement, a capital gains tax may have been due at the time of the transfer, even though no money traded hands (a tax on the profit made through the purchase and sale of an asset). Now, such transfers are considered non-taxable gifts between spouses and no capital gains tax becomes due at the time of the transfer. The spouse receiving the property assumes the previous capital gain, but will not be responsible for paying taxes on it until the property is actually sold and then only if the previous gain remains. It is important that the marital settlement agreement identify the property being transferred and state that it is a gift.

When jointly owned property is sold, such as the marital home, the spouses need to agree upon their respective responsibilities for any capital gains taxes which may be due and this agreement should be specified in the marital settlement agreement. Again, there are two ways to defer or eliminate capital gains taxes when the marital home is sold. If a spouse reinvests the gain in another residence within two years, the first gain is rolled over into the succeeding property. At age 55, a capital gains exemption applies which at this writing is $125,000. Sometimes couples wait until one of the spouses has reached his or her 55th birthday before the marital home is sold in order to take advantage of this exemption.

Property Settlements As Alimony

The Internal Revenue Service takes a very dim view of property settlements being treated as tax deductible alimony. This is sometimes considered when a husband agrees to pay his wife X amount of money if she relinquishes some or all of her interests in marital property. For example, a wife may have an interest in certain property belonging to her husband. He in turn may offer to pay wife $500 per month tax deductible alimony if she agrees to relinquish her interest in the property. New rules have redefined the meaning of alimony expressly to discourage property settlements from being treated in this manner. Couples are highly cautioned about attempting to have property settlements treated as tax deductible alimony.

We note, however, that this area should be reconsidered by Congress. In an effort to discourage property settlements from being treated as tax deductible alimony, the new rules also impede the creation of legitimate rehabilitative alimony plans. These plans provide for the payment of greater sums of alimony in their early years while a wife is re-entering the workforce or improving her job related skills. The new rules do not distinguish between legitimate rehabilitative alimony plans and property transfers made to look like tax deductible alimony. We think this is an appropriate area for Congress to review.

The Deductibility of Alimony Payments

Under the new law, spouses can decide whether or not spousal support payments will be tax deductible to the payor. However, if the spouses want the payments to be tax deductible to the payor (and therefore taxable income to the payee) certain requirements must be met. In order for payments to be deductible as alimony, they must be in cash, must not be required to be paid after the payee's death, and (if in excess of $10,000 in any year) must be paid for at least six years. The marital settlement agreement must specifically state that the payor has no continuing obligation to make payments after the death of the payee. We further recommend that the marital settlement agreement clearly state that the payments will be treated as tax deductible by the payor and will be treated as taxable income by the payee.

Some of these rules are those which discourage rehabilitative alimony plans. We object to the requirement that alimony must be paid for at least six years if the payments exceed $10,000 in any year. Often, it is appropriate for a spousal support plan to be effective for less than six years in amounts greater than $10,000 per year. It is also often appropriate for greater amounts to be paid in the early years of an alimony plan with gradual decreases occurring until the plan terminates. Under the new rules, these plans are not possible if the spouses want to make the payments tax deductible to the payor.

The Non-Deductibility of Child Support

Child support payments made by one spouse to the other may not be tax deductible to the payor. Under previous law, such payments could be tax-deductible if the marital settlement agreement was carefully drafted. Now, however, it is presumed that payments which terminate upon a child's reaching the age of majority (or on any other basis relating to a child) are strictly child support and are, therefore, non-deductible child support. Of course, child support payments made to a spouse are not considered taxable income.

Child Dependency Income Tax Exemptions

Under the new law, the Internal Revenue Service presumes that the custodial parent is the parent entitled to the exemption. In order for the non-custodial parent to claim the exemption, he or she must attach a waiver from the custodial parent to his or her income tax return (we believe this may be accomplished by attaching the appropriate page from the marital settlement agreement each year). What the law does not contemplate are those agreements which provide for joint custody or shared custody and further what the spouses should do if they agree to alternate the right to the exemption each year (as is often agreed upon). We suggest that the marital settlement agreement clearly contain the parties understanding regarding income tax exemptions relating to children and that this page be attached to the income tax return of the spouse who will be claiming the exemption for any particular year.

Child Care Tax Credits and Medical Expense Deductions For Children

Child care tax credits can be claimed by the custodial parent even if that parent is not taking the tax exemption for the child. However, the parent claiming the credit must have custody for more than half the year and provide more than half the financial support. Again, the new law does not provide for those situations where physical custody is shared on an essentially equal basis. We suggest that the agreement specifically set forth the parents agreements about the cost of child care as well as who will be considered the spouse entitled to claim any appropriate child care credit.

With regard to medical expense deductions for children, both parents may deduct such sums as each actually paid for a child's medical care (providing such expenses exceed 5%, together with any other medical expenses of the payor's adjusted gross income). It does not matter which parent will claim the child as an exemption.

Head of Household Status

Head of household tax status is often an overlooked tax advantage to the person who is otherwise entitled to it. Tax rates are not as high as those of a single taxpayer, but not as low as those for married couples filing joint returns. Therefore, it is most important, that single persons who are entitled to this status take it. Moreover, the custodial parent can still obtain Head of Household status, even though he or she has surrendered the dependency exemption.

In order to qualify for Head of Household status, you 1) must be unmarried, 2) your home must have been the principal place of residence for an unmarried child, or a child's descendant, or any relative, 3) you must have maintained your home for at least six months during the year in which the status is claimed, 4) you must have contributed over half the cost of maintaining such home.

Transfers of Retirement Benefits in Divorce and Waivers of Retirement Rights

Whenever either spouse has an interest in a retirement plan, the spouses must decide how the interest of the non-participating spouse in the plan will be treated. Typically, there are two methods of approach. First, the participating spouse may purchase the interest of the non-participating spouse. When this occurs, the non-participating spouse must appropriately waive his or her interest in the retirement plan. The plan administrator must be contacted to determine how this will be done. Second, the participating spouse may assign a part of the benefits of the plan to the non-participating spouse, to be distributed when the benefits are normally paid. The marital settlement agreement must specify the name and address of the participating spouse, and the name and address of the person who is designated as an alternate payee (the non-participating spouse). The agreement must specify the amount or percentage of the participant's benefits to be paid to each alternate payee or the manner in which the amount or percentage is to be determined, and the number of payments or the period during which the payments will be paid.

THE AGREEMENT

Beth and Dave Malone have now completed their mediation effort. They have both had the proposed Marital Settlement Agreement reviewed by their own attorneys. The agreement was found to be fair, legally sufficient and consistent with state law. Neither attorney had any significant objections to the agreement, but each had some suggestions as to the precise wording of certain provisions. After each attorney had had an opportunity to review the agreement, and to exchange their proposed language changes, Beth and Dave signed the agreement. We again caution our readers: this agreement is for example only. Do not make personal use of it.

Below, we set forth the *Marital Settlement Agreement* of Beth and Dave Malone.

MARITAL SETTLEMENT AGREEMENT

This agreement is entered into this 10th day of November, 1982, by and between Beth R. Malone (Wife) and David G. Malone (Husband).

Explanatory Statement

The parties were married by a religious ceremony on June 13, 1966 in Baltimore City, Maryland. As a result of their marital relationship, two children were born to them who are Christine A. Malone, born October 19, 1968, and Billy D. Malone, born August 3, 1971. Differences have arisen between the parties and they are now and have been since September 1, 1983, living separate and apart from one another, voluntarily and by mutual consent, in separate abodes, without cohabitation, with the purpose and intent of ending their marriage. It is the mutual desire of the parties in this agreement to formalize their voluntary separation and to settle questions of maintenance and support, alimony, counsel fees, their respective rights in the property or estate of the other, and in property owned by them jointly or as tenants by the entireties, and in marital property, and all other matters of every kind and character arising from their marital relationship.

NOW, THEREFORE, In consideration of the promises and mutual covenants and understandings of each of the parties, the parties hereby covenant and agree as follows, all as of the effective date hereof.

1. *Relinquishment of Marital Rights*

The parties shall continue to live separate and apart, free from interference, authority and control by the other, as if each were sole and unmarried, and each may conduct, carry on and engage in any employment, business or trade which to him shall seem advisable for his sole and separate use and benefit, without, and free from, any control, restraint, or interference by the other party in all respects as if each were unmarried. Neither of the parties shall molest or annoy the other or seek to compel the other to cohabit or dwell with him by any proceedings for restoration of conjugal rights or otherwise, or exert or demand any right to reside in the home of the other.

2. *Rights Incident to Marriage Relation and Rights As Surviving Spouse*

Except as otherwise provided herein, each of the parties hereto for himself or herself and his or her respective heirs, personal representatives and assigns, grants, remises and releases to the other, any and all rights or interest which he now has or may hereafter acquire in the real, personal or other property of the other. Each of the parties agrees to execute and deliver any and all deeds, releases, quit claims, or other instruments as from time to time may be necessary or convenient to enable the other party to deal with his property as if he were unmarried. Each of the parties releases all claims and demands of any kind or nature against the other party, including all interests incident to the marriage relation now or at any time hereafter existing or occurring in the property or estate of the other party, or in marital property, either statutory or arising at common law, specifically including all claims, demands, and interests arising under "Chapter 794 (1978) Laws of Maryland" and specifically including any right to act as the other's personal representative. It is the intention of each and both parties that during their respective lifetimes they may deal with their separate estates as if they were unmarried and that upon the death of either, the property, both real and personal, then owned by him shall pass by his will or under the laws of descent as the case might be, free from any right of inheritance, title or claim in the other party as if the parties at such time were unmarried.

3. *Marital Property and the Marital Home*

The parties have carefully reviewed all of their assets and have identified which are marital property. For the purposes of this agreement, marital property is all property acquired by either spouse during the marriage relationship other than property which was acquired by gift or inheritance by one spouse and not the other. After a thorough review of all marital property assets, the parties agree that their marital estate, as of the date of separation, had a value of $60,000, other than the marital home. Part of the marital estate consisted of Husband's pension. As of the date of separation, the parties agree that the pension had a value of $10,000.

At the time of the signing of this document, Beth Malone shall receive as her sole and separate property, the sum of $25,000 in cash. Excluding a division of the proceeds which will be derived from the sale of the marital home, the payment to Beth Malone of $25,000 represents a full and final settlement between the parties of their respective property interests.

The parties have agreed to place their marital home located at 1212 Clarks Road, Baltimore, Maryland, on the market for the purposes of expeditious sale. Until the house is actually sold and settlement occurs, Dave Malone shall continue to maintain the marital home as his primary place of residence. Upon the sale of the marital home, the parties shall equally divide all profits derived from the marital home. Until such sale, Dave Malone shall assume all financial responsibilities relating to the marital home.

During the course of mediation, the parties undertook a thorough review of each of their assets prior to the marriage relationship. The parties agree that they each brought essentially equal assets to the marriage relationship and therefore, neither party was given a credit for such premarital assets from marital property.

4. *Personal Property*

Prior to the execution of this agreement, the parties divided up their personal property. The parties agree that all tangible personal property and household chattels presently located at Wife's residence shall be and remain the sole and exclusive property of Wife, free and clear of any interest of Husband, and all tangible personal property and household chattels presently located at Husband's residence shall be and remain the sole and exclusive property of Husband, free and clear of any interest of Wife. Each party shall retain, as his or her sole and separate property, any automobiles, stocks, bonds or other securities, savings or checking accounts, and other assets of any kind or nature in his or her own name, free and clear of any interest of the other.

5. *Debts*

Husband shall assume all responsibility for the payment of charge account debts which occurred during the marriage relationship. All other debts, if any, shall be the responsibility of the spouse who contracted for them. Each spouse shall hold and save the other harmless from any and all liability therefor. From and after the date of this agreement, Husband and Wife covenant and agree that they will not pledge or attempt to pledge the credit of the other, nor will they contract or attempt to contract any debts or obligations in the name, or on behalf of each other, and as to any debts or obligations incurred or contracted by them from and after the date of this agreement, each will be responsible for his or her own debt or liability, and shall hold and save the other harmless, and indemnify the other, from any such debts or obligations.

6. *Income Tax Returns*

The parties shall file joint Federal and State income tax returns for the calendar year 1982. Husband agrees to pay the cost of preparing the tax returns. Husband and Wife agree to assume responsibility for the taxes due thereon, pro rata, in the same proportion that their respective separate incomes bear to the total gross income for federal income tax purposes in such year, making whatever adjustments between themselves as are necessary to reflect withholding, any balances due, and/or refunds; and each party will save and hold the other party harmless of and from all claims for taxes, interest, additions to taxes, penalties and expenses in connection with his own income and deductions.

7. *Grounds for Divorce*

At the time this Marital Settlement Agreement was executed, the parties agree that they shall procure a divorce on the basis of a twelve month voluntary separation. Notwithstanding such an agreement, the parties understand that neither party waives any right which they may have to obtain a divorce on any other grounds recognized by the laws of this state.

8. *Support*

Husband shall pay to Wife for her support and maintenance and for the support and maintenance of Christine Malone and Billy Malone, the annual sum of $19,800 in equal monthly installments of $1,650. These payments shall continue for a period of forty months, at which time support payments shall be reduced from the sum of $19,800 per year to the sum of $7,800 per year, payable in equal monthly installments of $650 per month. This sum shall continue to be paid by Husband to Wife so long as both Christine and Billy Malone continue to reside with her, and neither has reached his eighteenth birthday. When each child reaches his eighteenth birthday, the support payments provided for above, shall be reduced by the sum of $200 per month, so that upon both children reaching the age of eighteen, Husband shall make support payments to Wife in the amount of $250 per month. These payments shall continue until one of the following shall occur: (1) Husband or Wife dies; (2) The remarriage of Wife.

Husband and Wife understand that under the terms of the above spousal support and alimony plan, the payments made by Husband to Wife shall be deductible to Husband on his income tax returns. The parties further understand that the support payments provided for herein shall be considered taxable income to Wife and that she shall report same on her income tax returns each year.

9. *Custody*

Wife shall have the physical care and custody of the couple's two children, Christine and Billy Malone. In this regard, Wife shall be responsible for the day-to-day decisions affecting the health and welfare of her children. Husband and Wife have further agreed to the specific living arrangements of Christine and Billy Malone as it is their mutual desire that as far as is practically possible, they shall share equally time spent with their children. In this regard, each child shall have an overnight with Husband one weekday night per week. Husband may elect to have the children simultaneously for the overnight stay. Husband shall also have the right to have each child three weekends per month, comprised of one weekend night and one weekend day. Husband may elect to have the children simultaneously during these periods. During one weekend each month, Husband shall have the right to have both children stay with him for the entire weekend. Furthermore, Husband and Wife agree to work cooperatively in order to achieve a fair balancing of access time to their children during the following holidays: Thanksgiving, Christmas, Easter and the Fourth of July. Husband and Wife agree to discuss with each other the precise scheduling of visitation as previously set forth.

Husband and Wife further agree to adopt the principles of joint legal custody. In this regard, they agree to establish a cooperative relationship with each other regarding the exercise of their continuing responsibilities as parents of their children. They accept, that with respect to such matters as education, health care and religious training, each has an equal right to participate in those decisions affecting their children. Husband and Wife agree that in the event they are unable to make mutual and joint decisions with respect to the joint custody relationship of their children, they shall seek the services of a trained professional counselor or mediator, in order to help them reach mutually acceptable decisions affecting their children's welfare.

Husband and Wife agree that, should Wife plan any relocation from her immediate area of residence which would have the effect of impeding Husband's reasonable access to their children, Wife shall notify Husband of said plans and Husband and Wife agree to reopen negotiations with respect to custody and parental access arrangements.

10. *College Education*

Husband and Wife both acknowledge a desire for their children to obtain a higher education. Husband and Wife agree to mutually participate in the financial responsibilities associated with their children attending college, and will divide the costs of such educations between them *pro rata* to their respective net incomes at such time.

11. *Mutual Release and Hold Harmless*

Subject to and except for the provisions of this agreement, each party is released and discharged and by this agreement does for himself or herself, and his or her heirs, legal representatives, executors, administrators and assigns, release and discharge the other of and from all causes of action, claims, rights or demands, whatsoever in law or equity, which either of the parties ever had or now has against the other, except **for** the causes of action for divorce specified in Paragraph No. 7 above. Except as provided for in this agreement, neither party shall incur any liability on behalf of the other or make any charge against any account on which the other is liable, and each party covenants and agrees to indemnify the other and save him or her harmless from any liability for any obligations incurred by him or her in accordance with this agreement.

12. *Counsel Fees/Court Costs*

Each of the parties shall pay his or her own counsel fees incurred in connection with their separation and divorce. Each party hereby waives the right to assert any claim against the other party for counsel fees for legal services rendered to him or her at any time in the past, present or future. If a divorce proceeding is brought by either party against the other, the parties shall divide all court costs thereof, including any Master's fee, equally between them.

13. *Miscellaneous*

A. Each of the parties agrees to execute such other and further instruments and to perform such acts as may be reasonably required to effectuate the purposes of this agreement.

B. Except as otherwise provided herein, each of the parties hereto for himself or herself, and his or her respective heirs, personal representatives, and assigns, releases all claims, demands, and interests arising under the Marital Property Act, Chapter 794 (1978) Laws of Maryland, including but not limited to any claim to use and possession of the family home, if any; any claim to marital property; and any claim to a monetary award as an adjustment of the equities and rights of the parties concerning marital property, if any.

C. With the approval of any court of competent jurisdiction in which any divorce proceedings between the parties may be instituted at any time in the future, this agreement shall be incorporated in said decree of divorce. In the event the court shall fail or decline to incorporate this agreement or any provision thereof in said decree, then and in that event, the parties for themselves and their respective heirs, personal representatives and assigns, agree that they will nevertheless abide by and carry out all of the provisions hereof.

D. The parties mutually agree that in entering into this agreement, each party signs this agreement freely and voluntarily for the purpose and with the intent of fully settling and determining all of their respective rights and obligations growing out of or incident to their marriage. The parties achieved this agreement through mediation. The agreement was then independently reviewed by counsel for each spouse prior to its execution, or each spouse voluntarily and knowingly waived such review.

E. Whenever the masculine gender is used herein, it shall also mean the feminine gender, where appropriate, and the plural shall mean the singular, and vice-versa, where appropriate.

F. This agreement contains the entire understanding between the parties. No modification or waiver of any of the terms of this agreement shall be valid unless made in writing and signed by the parties.

G. As to these covenants and promises, the parties hereto severally bind themselves, their heirs, personal representatives and assigns.

H. Husband and Wife acknowledge that they have fully disclosed all their property, assets and liabilities to each other. They agree that a material basis for this agreement has been full disclosure by each and that this agreement shall be voidable in the event full disclosure has not been made.

_____ _____(SEAL)
WITNESS   BETH R. MALONE

_____ _____(SEAL)
WITNESS   DAVID G. MALONE

SOME FINAL THOUGHTS

The experiences of Beth and Dave Malone have helped us illustrate certain features of mediation. Their negotiations were, of course, fictitious and at times simplistic. Our readers should not necessarily apply any of the Malone's specific solutions to their own situation. Yet, we hope that the Malone's were able to convey "a sense" that disputes need not be resolved on the legal battlefield, and that two people who wish to do so can successfully resolve their differences rationally and intelligently.

With this in mind, it is our hope to facilitate the practice of divorce mediation to the greatest extent possible. To accomplish this, certain information and services will be provided to members of the general public. Below are listed two situations in which we might be helpful. If you wish to contact us about either of these situations, please write:

Parting Sense
c/o Greenspring Publications
#3 Barstad Court
Lutherville, Maryland 21093

1. You may have need for divorce mediation services and are interested in learning who practices divorce mediation in your community.
2. You believe you have the necessary qualifications to become a divorce mediator and are interested in obtaining information about mediation training.

Divorce is never an easy process. What is known with certainty, however, is that the emotional pain and financial cost of divorce is needlessly intensified by a legal system improperly entrusted with what is an essentially human, not legal event. This unnecessary suffering must stop. Mediation is now a proven way of treating divorce with the compassion, sensitivity and intelligence that it so desperately deserves. Mediation merits your serious consideration.

APPENDIX A
MEDIATION AGREEMENT

1. This agreement is made this ___ day of _____, 198__, between _____, divorce mediator, and _____.

2. It is made for the purpose of securing the professional services of a divorce mediator and for no other purpose. Divorce mediation is understood to be "a process of direct negotiations between the spouses in a terminating marriage in which a neutral mediator participates by exercising such skills and knowledge as will aid the spouses in reaching fair and equitable agreements relating to the following matters (or such of them as apply):

> Division of Property,
> Spousal Support,
> Child Custody and Parental Access,
> Child Support, and
> Tax Considerations.

Divorce mediation specifically excludes legal representation, marriage counseling or psychotherapy."

3. For the purposes of mediation, the spouses agree to adopt the guidelines attached hereto relating to division of marital property, spousal support, child custody and parental access and child support.

4. The fee for the mediation service shall be ___ per hour (including the drafting of documents). The spouses agree to share equally in responsibility for the fee or they agree to _____.

Payment for mediation services shall be made promptly after each session or upon billing, as the case may be.

5. The parties agree that upon the successful completion of a proposed marital settlement agreement, each spouse shall consult independently with private legal counsel to review the proposed agreement for legal sufficiency, or will knowingly and voluntarily waive such review. The mediator recommends such review.

6. The parties agree that during the mediation process, all matters in discussion shall be treated as strictly confidential and neither spouse shall consult with any other person about such matters, subject to paragraph seven (7) below.

7. The parties understand that during the mediation process, it may become necessary and appropriate to secure the professional services of other persons (tax accountants, appraisers, etc.). The spouses shall mutually choose such person, and it shall be the sole responsibility of the spouses to pay for any such services rendered.

8. The spouses agree that neither spouse will speak or communicate with the mediator about any of the matters subject to mediation unless both spouses are present.

9. The spouses agree to make full disclosure of all relevant financial and other data and documents, as necessary. The spouses further understand that the proposed marital settlement agreement shall contain a warranty that full financial disclosure has been made and that the agreement is voidable in the event that full disclosure has not been made.

Appendix A

10. The spouses agree that during the mediation process, neither spouse will transfer, sell or otherwise encumber any property in which they jointly or individually have an interest, without the knowledge and consent of the other spouse.

11. The spouses agree that if at any time they shall become involved in litigation concerning their divorce or separation, they hereby waive any right to involve the mediator in said litigation and further agree that nothing said or any acts done during the mediation process will be used for any purpose in litigation. This paragraph shall not apply to a voluntary separation agreement, should Husband and Wife enter such an agreement.

_____   _____
MEDIATOR

_____   _____

APPENDIX B
GUIDELINES

A. Guidelines for Division of Property

The parties shall reach agreement providing for the division of marital property with the assistance of the mediators, without regard to marital misconduct, in such proportions as is just, after considering all relevant factors, including:

    a. The contribution of each spouse to the acquisition of the marital property, including the contribution of a spouse as homemaker.

    b. The value of the property to be received or retained by each spouse.

    c. The economic circumstances of each spouse at the time the division of property is to become effective, including the desirability of awarding the family home or the right to live therein for reasonable periods to the spouse having custody of any children.

    d. Any increases or decreases in the values of the separate property of each spouse during the marriage or the depletion of the separate property for marital purposes.

    e. For purposes of this section:

        Active ownership of property is inferred from the owner's making capital improvements, usage, management, and other efforts intended to enhance the value of the property.

        Passive ownership is inferred from the absence of factors which would result in an inference of active ownership.

Marital property means all property acquired by either spouse subsequent to the marriage except:
(1) Property acquired by gift, bequest, devise, or descent.
(2) Property acquired in exchange for property acquired by gift, bequest, devise, or descent.
(3) Property acquired by a spouse after a decree of legal separation.
(4) Property excluded by valid agreement of the parties.
(5) The increase in value resulting from passive ownership of property acquired prior to the marriage, or after the marriage by gift, bequest, devise, or descent.
(6) When increases in value of property acquired prior to the marriage, after the marriage or by gift, bequest, devise, or descent have resulted from both active and passive ownership, a reasonable allocation shall be made so as to exclude increases attributable to passive ownership.

f. All property acquired by either spouse after the marriage prior to a decree of legal separation or divorce and all increases in value attributable to active ownership of property whenever or however acquired, are presumed to be marital property regardless of whether title is held individually or by the spouses in some form of coownership, such as joint tenancy, tenancy in common, tenancy by the entirety, and community property. The presumption of marital property shall be overcome by a showing that the property increase or value of property is excluded under the provisions of the preceding subsection.

g. Property shall be valued for purposes of this section as of the date of the first mediation session.

B. Spousal Maintenance Guidelines

Payment of maintenance by one spouse to the other shall be predicated upon the following considerations as they apply to the spouse seeking maintenance:

a. The spouse lacks sufficient property, including marital property apportioned to him, to provide for his reasonable needs.

b. The spouse is fully or partially unable to support himself through appropriate employment or is the custodian of a child whose condition or circumstances make it appropriate that the custodian not be required to seek employment outside the home.

c. Maintenance shall be in such amounts and for such periods of time as it just, without regard to marital misconduct and after considering all relevant factors, including the following:

>(1) The financial resources of the party seeking maintenance, including marital property apportioned to him, and his ability to meet his needs independently, including the extent to which a provision for support of a child living with the party includes a sum for that party as custodian.

(2) The time necessary to acquire sufficient education or training to enable the party seeking maintenance to find appropriate employment.

(3) The standard of living established during the marriage, reduced by the impact that maintaining two households rather than one may have upon the standard of living of the parties.

(4) The duration of the marriage.

(5) The age and physical and emotional condition of each spouse.

(6) The ability of the spouse from whom maintenance is sought to meet his needs while meeting those of the spouse seeking maintenance.

C. Child Support Guidelines

Either parent or both parents, according to their ability to do so, shall accept the duty of support for a child of the marriage and contribute an amount reasonably necessary after considering all relevant factors, including:

a. The financial resources of the child.

b. The earning ability and financial resources of each parent.

c. The standard of living the child would have enjoyed had the marriage not been dissolved, reduced by the impact that maintaining two households rather than one may have upon the standard of living of the parties.

d. The physical and emotional condition of the child and his educational needs.

D. Child Custody Guidelines

In reaching agreement regarding custodial arrangements reflecting the best interests of the child, the parties shall consider all relevant factors, including:

    a. The wishes of each parent as to the custody of the child.

    b. The wishes of the child as to custodial arrangements.

    c. The interaction and interrelationship with his parent or parents, his siblings, and any other person who may significantly affect the child's best interests.

    d. The child's adjustment to his home, school, and community.

    e. The mental and physical health of all individuals involved.

The conduct of a parent that does not demonstrably affect his relationship with the child, or in some other way can be shown to be contrary to the best interests of the child, shall not be considered.

E. Parental Access and Responsibilities

Rights of the Custodial Parent. The custodial parent may determine the child's upbringing, including his education, health care, and religious training, except as otherwise agreed by the parties. The custodial parent shall have the right to require that the noncustodial parent follow agreed visitation with the children on a consistent and dependable basis.

Rights of the Noncustodial Parent. The noncustodial parent of the child shall be entitled to reasonable visitation rights such as do not adversely affect the child's education or physical health or significantly impair his emotional development. The noncustodial parent shall carry out visitation arrangements as a privilege and obligation of parenthood and to share parenting responsibility with the custodial parent.

Rights of Joint Custodial Parents. To the extent that the spouses agree to joint custody, joint custodial parents shall establish a cooperative relationship with each other regarding the exercise of their continuing responsibilities as parents of their children. They accept that each has an equal right to determine the child's upbringing, including his education, health care, and religious training. The child's living arrangements between the two parents shall be such as are in the best interests of the child, using as guidelines the provisions of "D" herein. Even though joint custody reflects a cooperative attitude on the part of both parents, specific living arrangements shall be included in the settlement agreement. Such arrangements shall be followed except as are otherwise agreed upon by the parents from time to time.

APPENDIX C
TRIAL SEPARATION AGREEMENT

1. This agreement is made this ___ day of _____, 1983, by and between DAVID MALONE (Husband) and BETH MALONE (Wife).

2. The purpose of this agreement is to permit the parties to live separate and apart, as hereinafter provided, without either of them relinquishing any of their marital rights or responsibilities. The parties expressly agree that their trial separation shall not be a basis to be used by either of them for the purpose of achieving a grounds for divorce. The consideration for this agreement is the mutual promises and covenants made by Husband and Wife.

3. The goal of this trial separation is to permit both parties to decide whether their marriage shall continue or will be dissolved by virtue of a future formal separation and divorce proceeding.

4. The parties agree that during the term of this agreement they shall not cohabit with any other person, nor will they date or have sexual relations with a third party.

5. The term of this agreement shall be four weeks beginning with the date it is signed.

6. The parties jointly own a house and property located at 1212 Clark's Road, Baltimore, Maryland. Furthermore, the parties are the parents of two children who are Chris and Billy Malone.

7. Beginning with the date this trial separation agreement is signed, Husband shall make arrangements to reside for a period of one month, at a place other than the marital home. In the event Husband desires to reenter the marital home for any reason during the one month period that this agreement shall be in effect, he shall call Wife in advance and notify her of his desire to reenter the marital home. Wife shall not deny Husband such access.

8. Husband and Wife acknowledge and agree that it is of paramount importance that both Husband and Wife continue to have close, continuing contact with their two children during the period of this trial separation. In this regard, Husband shall spend one full day each weekend with both children and, in addition, shall spend two evenings per week with both children. The specific arrangements for such visitation and access will be worked out between Husband and Wife.

9. Husband and Wife acknowledge that they have sufficient income to continue paying the household expenses during the time of this trial separation agreement. In this regard, Wife shall continue to pay the household expenses from the couple's joint checking account and Husband shall deposit $300 per week into said checking account.

10. The parties agree that during the period when this trial separation agreement is in effect, neither shall institute any legal proceedings against the other.

11. The parties further agree that Husband and Wife will actively participate in a marriage counseling process during the period of this trial separation. These counseling

sessions will occur at least once every week, jointly, or as needed individually.

12. The parties further agree that Husband and Wife will allocate, once per week, time that they will spend together without interruption. The length of this time period will be negotiated each week by both parties depending on their respective schedules.

13. During the course of this trial separation, the parties agree that they shall not discuss the subject of separation and divorce.

_____   _____
    DAVID MALONE   BETH MALONE

APPENDIX D
TEMPORARY SEPARATION AGREEMENT

1. This agreement is made this ___ day of _____, 1983, by and between DAVID MALONE (Husband), and BETH MALONE (Wife).

2. It is made for the purpose of providing temporary settlement of property; spousal support; living arrangements and support of minor children; and visitation of said children. It in no way influences the final settlement which will be agreed upon during the mediation process.

3. The parties agree that on the first day of September, 1983, they began living separate and apart from one another, voluntarily, and by mutual consent, in separate abodes, without cohabitation, with the purpose and intent of ending their marriage.

4. Husband and Wife own a house and property located at 1212 Clark's Road, Baltimore, Maryland. Husband and Wife agree that this home will be the primary place of residence for their children, Chris and Billy Malone, during the period of time this temporary settlement agreement remains in effect. Husband and Wife further agree that they shall alternate living in the house with their children on a weekly basis. The parent not living in the house during any given week shall have the right to spend two evenings per week with the couple's two children.

5. Husband shall pay to Wife for her support the sum of $500 per month. In addition, Husband shall be responsible

for the payment of the mortgage on the marital home, utilities on the marital home, and all food to be consumed in the marital home. Husband shall also assume all other regular and customary expenses, such as automobile insurance which may come due during the time this temporary settlement agreement remains in effect.

    6. The consideration for this agreement is the mutual promises and obligations of Husband and Wife as described herein.

---------------------   ---------------------
DAVID MALONE   BETH MALONE

APPENDIX E
FINANCIAL INFORMATION

ATTACH COPIES OF FEDERAL INCOME TAX RETURNS FOR THE LAST THREE YEARS AND COPIES OF ALL FINANCIAL STATEMENTS FURNISHED TO BANKS OR OTHER CREDITORS DURING THE SAME PERIOD. The financial information called for on the following pages is important. If you need help in completing any item, please let your mediator know.

Assets

Estimate the value of each of the following items of property. If any item is located in a jurisdiction other than that in which you live, indicate where such item is located, and, if necessary, give details on a separate sheet. Indicate how much of each asset held in joint ownership was contributed by husband and how much by wife.

	Husband	Wife	Joint

A. Real Estate (home and other):

B. Bank and Savings Accounts:

C. Notes, Accounts Receivable
    (Money owed to you. Indicate by
    whom, amount, and date(s)
    payable):

    _____ ___ ___ ___
    _____ ___ ___ ___
    _____ ___ ___ ___

D. Stocks, Bonds, Mutual Funds:

    _____ ___ ___ ___
    _____ ___ ___ ___
    _____ ___ ___ ___

E. Life Insurance—Name of
    Company, Policy Number, Face
    Value, Type ("term," "whole
    life," etc.) and Location of Policy:

    _____ ___ ___ ___
    _____ ___ ___ ___
    _____ ___ ___ ___

F. Business or Professional Interests
    (please furnish last balance sheet
    and profit and loss statement,
    tax return, buy-sell agreements,
    etc.):

    _____ ___ ___ ___
    _____ ___ ___ ___
    _____ ___ ___ ___
    _____ ___ ___ ___

G. Miscellaneous Property (employee benefits, pensions—furnish last statement, descriptive booklet and information on vesting; stock options, patents, trademarks, copyrights, royalties, etc.):

_____ _____ _____ _____
_____ _____ _____ _____
_____ _____ _____ _____
_____ _____ _____ _____

H. Personal Effects, Automobile, Tangible Personal Property:

_____ _____ _____ _____
_____ _____ _____ _____
_____ _____ _____ _____
_____ _____ _____ _____

                         Total Assets _____ _____ _____

Liabilities

A. Mortgages on Real Estate:

_____ _____ _____ _____
_____ _____ _____ _____
_____ _____ _____ _____
_____ _____ _____ _____

B. Notes Payable to Banks and Others:

_____ _____ _____ _____
_____ _____ _____ _____
_____ _____ _____ _____
_____ _____ _____ _____

C. Loans on Insurance Policies:

_____ _____ _____ _____
_____ _____ _____ _____
_____ _____ _____ _____
_____ _____ _____ _____

D. Other Debts:

_____ _____ _____ _____
_____ _____ _____ _____
_____ _____ _____ _____
_____ _____ _____ _____
_____ _____ _____ _____

       Total Liabilities _____ _____ _____
  Net Worth (Assets — Liabilities) _____ _____ _____

Income Statement

If income is received *other than monthly*, such as annual bonuses or quarterly dividends, then state *all income and deductions* on an annual basis and divide the net amount by twelve.

	Husband	Wife
Gross Salary (annual or monthly)	_____	_____
Less: Withholding	_____	_____
FICA	_____	_____
Other Deductions (specify):		
_____	_____	_____
_____	_____	_____
Net Salary	_____	_____
Dividend Income*	_____	_____
Interest Income*	_____	_____

Appendix E

Income from Trusts*
Rental Income*
Other Income (specify):

Less Deductions for:
    Estimated Taxes
    Other Deductions (specify):

                      Total Deductions

    Net Annual (take home) Income

    Average Monthly Net Income
      (1/12th of Annual Figure)

---

*If this income is received jointly, so indicate and divide between husband and wife.

APPENDIX F
MONTHLY EXPENSE BUDGET

If you do not anticipate that the children of your present marriage will be living with you, complete only column A. If you anticipate that the children will be living with you, please attempt to distribute your estimated monthly needs between columns A and B. Some will be difficult, such as rent. On rent, for example, you may estimate what a residence for yourself alone would cost and list that cost in column A, then estimate the cost for yourself and the children, and list in column B the difference between that cost and the amount listed in column A. If you have questions about the distribution, please ask your mediator about it. The numbers in parentheses correspond to columns on "Analysis of Family Expenditures" Sheet.

ITEMS		A (Yourself)	B (Children)
Set-Asides:			
Emergencies and Future Goals (from Schedule A)	(1)	_____	_____
Seasonal Expenses (from Schedule B)	(2)	_____	_____
Regular Monthly Expenses:			
Housing			
Rent	(3)	_____	_____
House Payments			
Principal and Interest	(3)	_____	_____
Real Estate Taxes	(3)	_____	_____

Appendix F

Home Insurance	(3)	____ ____
Other (specify) _____	(3)	____ ____

Utilities
    Electricity (4) ____ ____
    Gas/Heating Oil (5) ____ ____
    Telephone (6) ____ ____
    Water (7) ____ ____
    Other (specify) _____ ____ ____

Installment Debt Payments
    (from Schedule C) (8) ____ ____

                        Total of Above ____ ____

Day-to-Day Expenses:

Food and Dairy
    At Home (9) ____ ____
    Away from Home (9) ____ ____

Clothing
    (including working clothes) (10) ____ ____

Transportation
    Gas and Oil (11) ____ ____
    Auto Repair & Maintenance (11) ____ ____
    Other (bus, taxi,
        parking, etc.) (11) ____ ____

Health, Medical, and Dental
    Medical, Dental & Hospital
        Insurance (12) ____ ____
    Medical & Health Care
        (not covered by insurance) (12) ____ ____
    Dental
        (not covered by insurance) (12) ____ ____
    Medicines & Drugs (12) ____ ____

Miscellaneous
   Repairs (13) _____ _____
   Garden or Yard Work (13) _____ _____
   Replacement of Furnishings (13) _____ _____
   Dry Cleaning & Laundry (13) _____ _____
   Domestic Help (___ days at
      $_____ per day) (13) _____ _____
   Children's Day Care (13) _____ _____
   Other (specify) _____ (13) _____ _____

Education, Self and Children
(Immediate Needs)
   Private School Tuition (14) _____ _____
   College Tuition (14) _____ _____
   Books and Fees (14) _____ _____
   Other (specify) _____ (14) _____ _____

Variable Monthly Expenses:
   Drug/Variety Store Items (15) _____ _____
   Books, Magazines, Newspapers (15) _____ _____
   Children's Allowances (15) _____ _____
   Charities, Gifts, Contributions (15) _____ _____
   Dues (Club or Professional
      not included as
      business expenses) (15) _____ _____
   Cultural/Recreational (15) _____ _____
   Other (specify) _____ (16) _____ _____
   _____ (17) _____ _____
   _____ (18) _____ _____
      Total Monthly Expenses _____ _____

Appendix F 127

SET-ASIDE
Emergencies and Future Goals
Schedule A

Type of Fund	Probable Cost	Date Desired	Amount to Set Aside This Year	Amount to Set Aside per Month
Emergency				
Savings				
Major Appliances and Equipment				
Home Improvement, Painting, Major Repair				
Education Self Children				
Auto Replacement				
Debt Retirement (other than installment)				
Investment				
Other (specify)				
TOTALS	$	XXX	$	$

Schedule B

Expense	Date Needed	AMOUNT Per Year	Per Month
Taxes (Auto Tags, Ad Valorum)			
Auto Insurance			
Life & Disability Insurance			
Vacation			
Other (specify)			
TOTALS	XXX	$	$

Regular Monthly Expenses
Installment Debt Payments

Schedule C

Name of Creditor	Balance Owed*	Amount of Monthly Payment	Date of Last Payment	Due Date of Next Payment**
Total Balance and Monthly Payments				
Total Delinquent Payments				

*Payment times remaining number of payments.
**If payments are delinquent, *due date of next payment* may be earlier than current date or even the date of last payment.

FOOTNOTES

CHAPTER ONE
1. Committee on the Family, Group for the Advancement of Psychiatry. *Divorce, Child Custody and the Family.* San Francisco: Jossey-Bass, 1981.
2. Pearson, J. and Thoennes, N. "Mediation and Divorce: The Benefits Outweigh the Costs," *The Family Advocate,* 1982, 4, 26-29.
3. Watts, Judge Robert B. *The Daily Record.* Baltimore: The Daily Record Co., September 30, 1981.

CHAPTER FIVE
1. Pearson, J. and Thoennes, N. "Mediation and Divorce: The Benefits Outweigh the Costs," *The Family Advocate,* 4, 26-29, 1982.

CHAPTER SIX
1. Committee on the Family, Group for the Advancement of Psychiatry. *Divorce, Child Custody and the Family.* San Francisco: Jossey-Bass, 1981.
2. Wallerstein, J. and Kelly, J. *Surviving the Breakup: How Children and Parents Cope with Divorce.* New York: Basic Books, 1980.
3. Haddad, W. and Roman, M. "No-Fault Custody," 2 *Family Law Review,* 95, 1979.
4. *Tuter v. Tuter,* 120 S.W. 2d 203, 205 (1938).
5. 1929 Maryland Laws, Chapter 561, Section 1.
6. *Watts v. Watts,* 350 N.Y.S. 2d 285, 290 (1973).

REFERENCES

BAHR, S. "An Evaluation of Court Mediation: A Comparison in Divorce Cases with Children," *Journal of Family Issues.* 2(1) : 39-60, 1981.

BENEDEK, E. and BENEDEK, R. "Joint Custody: Solution or Illusion," *American Journal of Psychiatry,* 136, 12, 1540-1544, 1979.

BENEDEK, R. and BENEDEK, E. "Children of Divorce: Can We Meet Their Needs?" *Journal of Social Issues,* 35(4) : 155-169, 1979.

Committee on the Family, Group for the Advancement of Psychiatry, *Divorce, Child Custody and the Family,* San Francisco: Jossey-Bass, 1981.

COOGLER, O. J., *Structured Mediation In Divorce Settlement.* Lexington: D. C. Heath, 1978.

ESTER, J. "Maryland Custody Law—Fully Committed to the Child's Best Interests," 41 Maryland Law Review 225 (1982).

FRAMO, J. "The Friendly Divorce," *Psychology Today,* February, 1978.

GARDNER, R. *Psychotherapy With Children of Divorce,* New York: Jason Aronson, Inc., 1976.

GARDNER, R. *The Boys and Girls Book About Divorce.* New York: Bantam Books, 1970.

GOLDSTEIN, J., FREUD, A. and SOLNIT, A. *Beyond The Best Interests Of the Child,* New York: The Free Press, 1973.

GREIF, J. "Fathers, Children and Joint Custody," *American Journal Of Orthopsychiatry,* 49 (2) : 311-319, 1979.

HADDAD, W. and ROMAN, M. "No-Fault Custody," *Family Law Review,* 95, 95, 1979.

HETHERINGTON, E., COX, M. and COX, R. "Beyond Father Absence: Conceptualization of Effects of Divorce," *Contemporary Readings in Child Psychology,* Hetherington, E. and Parke, R. New York: McGraw Hill, 1977.

KRANTZLER, M. *Creative Divorce,* New York: Lippincott, 1974.

LUEPNITZ, D. "Which Aspects of Divorce Affect Children?" *Family Coordinator*, 28(1) : 79-85, 1979.

McDERMOTT, J. "Parental Divorce in Early Childhood," *American Journal of Psychiatry*, 124, 10, 1424-1432, 1968.

MILLER, D. "Joint Custody," *Family Law Quarterly*, 13(3) : 345-412, 1979.

MORGENBESSER, M. and NEHLS, N. *Joint Custody: An Alternative For Divorcing Families*, Chicago: Nelson-Hall, 1981.

PEARSON, J. and THOENNES, N. "Mediation and Divorce: The Benefits Outweigh the Costs," *The Family Advocate*, 4, 26-29, 1982.

RUTTER, M. *The Quality of Mothering: Maternal Deprevation Reassessed*, England: Penguin Books, 1974.

ROMAN, M. and HADDAD, W. *The Disposable Parent.* New York: Holt, Reinhart and Winston, 1978.

SALK, L. *What Every Child Would Like Parents To Know About Divorce*, New York: Harper and Row, 1978.

SILVER, G. and SILVER, M. *Weekend Fathers*, Los Angeles: Stratford Press, 1981.

TROYER, W. *Divorced Kids*, Toronto: Clarke, Irwin and Co., 1979.

Tuter v. Tuter, 120 S.W. 2d 203, 205 (1938).

WALLERSTEIN, J. and KELLY, J. *Surviving the Breakup: How Children And Parents Cope With Divorce*, New York: Basic Books, 1980.

Watts v. Watts, 350 N.Y.S. 2d 285, 290 (1973).

WHEELER, M. *Divided Children: A Legal Guide for Divorcing Parents*, New York: W. W. Norton & Co., 1980.

INDEX

Index

Adversarial divorce
  fees 14
  time 14

Business, professional interests
  as marital property 41

Children
  effect of divorce on 71
  when best served 72

Child support
  as approached by
    mediation 69
  budget analysis 69
  college costs 70
  modifiable by courts 69
  non-payment of 69
  when paid 69

Courts
  right to modify decree 20

Custody
  history 73
  joint custody 74, 75
  maternal preference
    doctrine 73
  parental rights 74

Debts
  adjustment of 55
  mortgage loans 57
  retail credit accounts 56
  revolving charge accounts .. 56

Divorce
  emotional response 11
  fault as a basis for 12
  no-fault recognized 12

Divorce decree 17

Educational degree
  as marital property 43

Family home 44

Financial and information
  form purpose 59

Gifts 47

Health insurance 64

Household effects 48

Lawyers 11

Life insurance 43

Malone negotiations
  custody 76
  dividing marital property .. 50
  orientation session 16
  support 65
  temporary agreement 32

Marital property
  defined 29
  division of 49
  treatment in mediation ... 53

Marital settlement agreement
  as a contract 19
  Malone agreement 91

Marriage
  emotional investment in .. 10

Mediation
  agreement, example of ... 105
  changed circumstances ... 15
  co-mediation 26
  confidentiality 24
  conflict, minimization of .. 12
  definition for 8
  distinct process 21
  fees 14
  full disclosure 24
  functions, as to property .. 37
  guidelines 28, 108

initial session 13
joint v. shuttle 27
methods of 25
negotiations in 9
new approach 3
other uses for 10
purpose 9
rational cooperation 3
self-empowering 9
spouses, continuing contact 12
time, element of 14
use of lawyers 25

Mediator
  client agreement 28
  how to locate 103
  neutrality 23
  professional backgrounds .. 21
  purpose 21
  training as 103

Pensions
  as marital property 39
  how treated 40
  military, new law 39
  valuation of 40

Property
  identification of 37
  non-marital 38
  significance of 87

Real Estate
  as marital property 44

Spousal support
  approach in mediation 29
  budget review 62
  sample options 61

Tax matters
  capital gains 84
  property settlements as
    alimony 84
  the deductability of
    alimony 85
  dependency exemptions 87

Temporary separation
    agreement
  example of 117
  purposes of 31

Trial separation agreement
  example of 114

NOTES